What people are saying about …

A Friend in Me

"Am I in a relationship because I truly care about another woman—or because I want to check caring off my list of to-dos? Does my tone of voice really matter in a friendship? Pam pushes us past our blind spots to a more honest self-assessment and therefore more meaningful connection with the women in our lives, especially the younger ones we most want to love well."

Elisa Morgan, speaker and author
of *The Beauty of Broken*

"If you long to make a lasting difference in the lives of women in the next generation, read *A Friend in Me*. With raw honesty, poignant illustrations, and courageous action steps—all woven within biblical truth—Pamela Havey Lau has written a book that challenges women to be intentional about investing their time, influence, knowledge, and friendship in women. Don't miss this extraordinary book!"

Carol Kent, speaker and author of
Becoming a Woman of Influence

"Friendship with other women has been a powerful source of grace and sustenance in my life. With this book that is both practical and discipling, I hope friendship—with other women and with God—becomes this for you too."

Katelyn Beaty, managing editor of
Christianity Today magazine

"*A Friend in Me* is a must-read for any woman seeking to build meaningful relationships with the next generation of women. Transparent, yet practical, Pam Lau's message is filled with stories of hope and grace, passionately calling women to stand against the culture wars while humbly reaching out to the next generation of women. We urge you to read this book as you consider how you will pass along your faith in today's rapidly changing world."

Drs. Les and Leslie Parrott, authors of
Saving Your Marriage Before It Starts

"Having served as a pastor with youth and young adults for over twenty years, I cannot overstate the importance of intergenerational relationships and what Pam writes about in this book. Far too often in our contemporary Christian culture we isolate generations and we miss out on the beauty of the body of Christ and the wisdom and wonder of what happens when generations come together. I am personally very aware of this as in my life the three men who mentored me when I was in my twenties and thirties were ninety-two years old, eighty-three years old, and sixty-eight years old. I cannot imagine what my walk with Jesus would be like … if God had not placed these older men in my life. I am thrilled that Pam has written this book because so many lives will be changed if we heed the advice and biblical guidance she brings."

Dan Kimball, pastor of Vintage Faith Church
and author of *They Like Jesus but Not the Church*

"Pamela boldly calls women to reach out to younger women in friendship. *A Friend in Me* is a wonderful tool kit, inspiring courage, forgiveness, joy, and wisdom to flourish as we learn to hold each other in safe and loving embraces."

Lisa Graham McMinn, author of *Growing Strong Daughters* and *The Contented Soul*

"Pamela writes profoundly about the importance of allowing ourselves to be present in the lives of others. I have seen how true, deep relationships can affect the impact of the gospel as it moves through our cities, one person at a time. This is an honest look at our need for change and a hopeful testimony of what God longs to do in and through us."

Kevin Palau, president of Luis Palau Association

"As a woman who at one time yearned for an older woman to mentor and befriend me, I am enthusiastic about Pam Lau's book *A Friend in Me*. The need for younger-to-older-women friendships is more urgent now than ever before in our fractured and pluralistic culture. Younger women want the compassionate wisdom and care of an older woman friend. Pam makes the desire for such friendships crystal clear with compelling stories and research. Then she carefully unpacks all the important spiritual and practical truths that go along with making such a relationship trustworthy and helpful. Every woman who yearns for the companionship of someone a little ahead of her in the journey will love this book."

Dr. MaryKate Morse, author, mother, and friend to women

"I was captivated by the warm and practical description of mentor relationships and how important it is to mentor other women—no matter what age we are. Typical mentors offer lessons on the unwritten rules in the professional world, but great mentors focus on our whole life including faith, relationships, and work. Pamela also gets real on a topic that is rarely discussed authentically in the faith-based world … sex. I shared that chapter with my daughter and it helped me communicate effectively with her on an important topic."

Diane Paddison, founder of 4word
(www.4wordwomen.org) and
author of *Work, Love, Pray*

"After reading this book, I am motivated to be a safe haven for other women. *A Friend in Me* is refreshingly honest about the challenges of life and the need for meaningful friendships to face those challenges. Pamela Lau's candid transparency, gentle exhortation, and sage wisdom provide coaching to nurture and deepen cross-generational friendships between women."

Lindsay Olesberg, Scripture engagement
director at InterVarsity Christian Fellowship
and author of *The Bible Study Handbook*

"If you have found yourself disillusioned with the quality of real friendship with Christian women, Pam Lau offers deep wisdom that cuts to the heart of the crisis of loneliness in our churches and neighborhoods. Pam inspires us to pursue friendship with women in our lives with courageous vulnerability and compassion without judgment. This book makes me want to live more deeply and share life more raw and unfiltered with my women friends. I will share this book with my students, friends, and colleagues! Thank you, Pam, for investing your heart and soul into such a passionate and beautiful call to action!"

Dr. Sarah Thomas Baldwin, vice president
for student development at Asbury University

"From one generation to the next, women have been some of our very best teachers. The women who have gone before us have blessed us with a rich legacy to emulate and in which to find inspiration for daily living. Now, it's our turn. There are women looking up to us, who desire to have us speak wisdom into their lives and to lead well into the next generation. Will we be up to the task? Pamela Havey Lau uses captivating storytelling, anecdotal evidence, and sound biblical teaching to give women of today practical steps for becoming a safe place for our young women to work through their questions and everyday issues related to faith, friendships, relationships, family, and work. This is a recommended guidebook for building meaningful, face-to-face relationships with the next generation."

Deidra Riggs, managing editor
of TheHighCalling.org and author
of *Every Little Thing*

"This book is a powerful tool, pairing stories and principles to reimagine the way women of different ages and backgrounds can relate to one another. By offering a roadmap for women who desire to forge more intimate and authentic relationships with younger women, Pamela Havey Lau enables women to stand together as they navigate the challenging journey of life and faith. Pamela is a passionate, honest, comforting guide who, having turned her own despair into hope, credibly encourages others to do the same. She challenges readers to share their own stories with transparency, venerability, and humility in order to create space for young women to believe that their story is heard, understood, and valued. This book illuminates our need for intergenerational relationships, as we all sit, together, in the sacred presence of God."

Christena Cleveland, PhD, author of *Disunity in Christ: Uncovering the Hidden Forces That Keep Us Apart* and associate professor of reconciliation studies at Bethel University

"With the pressure on this generation of young women to do it all, we can unwittingly settle for shallow friendships along the way. Encouraging women to go deeper is a benefit to each of us and the church as a whole. Pam Havey Lau showcases how and why women in the church must look to one another for guidance, comfort, and a model of Christ's love. Her book is an impassioned guide for living out Titus 2 in the twenty-first century."

Kate Shellnutt, editor of *Christianity Today*'s Her.meneutics

"For many women today, life in our busy, fast-paced, social-media-driven world involves too many superficial interactions with acquaintances and few deep relationships with real friends, especially older friends who are a step or two ahead of us in life's journey. Christian women of all ages are longing for deep, life-giving friendships but are not sure how to cultivate the connections for which they yearn. With passion and keen insight, Pam Lau offers practical and biblically informed guidance to those who long to build sheltering relationships with younger women in their lives."

Rev. Robin R. Garvin, pastor of encouragement
at Lake Grove Presbyterian Church

a friend in me

how to be a
safe haven for other women

pamela havey lau

David C Cook®
transforming lives together

A FRIEND IN ME
Published by David C Cook
4050 Lee Vance View
Colorado Springs, CO 80918 U.S.A.

David C Cook Distribution Canada
55 Woodslee Avenue, Paris, Ontario, Canada N3L 3E5

David C Cook U.K., Kingsway Communications
Eastbourne, East Sussex BN23 6NT, England

The graphic circle C logo is a registered trademark of David C Cook.

The website addresses recommended throughout this book are offered as a
resource to you. These websites are not intended in any way to be or imply an
endorsement on the part of David C Cook, nor do we vouch for their content.

Unless otherwise noted, all Scripture quotations are taken from the Holy Bible,
New International Version®, NIV®. Copyright © 1973, 2011 by Biblica, Inc.™ Used
by permission of Zondervan. All rights reserved worldwide. www.zondervan.com.
Scripture quotations marked ESV are taken from The Holy Bible, English Standard
Version® (ESV®), copyright © 2001 by Crossway, a publishing ministry of Good
News Publishers. Used by permission. All rights reserved; MSG are taken from *THE
MESSAGE*. Copyright © by Eugene H. Peterson 1993, 2002. Used by permission of
NavPress Publishing Group; and VOICE are taken from *The Voice Bible* Copyright ©
2012 Thomas Nelson, Inc. The Voice™ translation © 2012 Ecclesia Bible Society. All
rights reserved. The author has added italics to Scripture quotations for emphasis.

LCCN 2014957979
ISBN 978-1-4347-0864-9
eISBN 978-1-4347-0931-8

© 2015 Pamela Havey Lau
Published in association with literary agent Heidi Mitchell of D.C. Jacobson &
Associates LLC, an Author Management Company. www.dcjacobson.com.

The Team: Ingrid Beck, Liz Heaney, Nick Lee, Jack Campbell, Karen Athen
Cover Design: Amy Konyndyk
Cover Photo: iStock

Printed in the United States of America
First Edition 2015

1 2 3 4 5 6 7 8 9 10

033015

To the Next Generation:
Michaela Brynn Lau
Annalise Havey Lau
Gabrielle Elizabeth Lau
Lauren Ruth Knapp
Ava Elizabeth Pulliam

There is only one cure for the malady that afflicts our culture, and that is to speak the truth about it. Once we can bring ourselves to do that, it will be time to worry about "constructive solutions," "practical proposals" and "social alternatives" for our young—discussion of which, so long as it is so absurdly premature, serves only to distract our attention from the truth about ourselves.

Christopher Lasch

For discussion videos and questions on the key points of this book, go to www.pamelalau.com/videos.

Contents

Foreword

I remember, years ago, hearing a woman talk to a group of young mothers, encouraging and challenging them in this deeply important role that was simultaneously rewarding and difficult. I felt an ache rise in me that seemed out of place. I wasn't sure what it was about, but I gave it time and space and, within just a few minutes, I realized I was thinking, *Where was someone like her when I was their age?*

The longing for a mentor, for someone who has gone on the journey before you and stops, or at least slows down, and takes the time to walk alongside of you, is a rare thing. I think Pam is that kind of person. She deftly describes the unfortunate chasm that can arise between generations of women and then, slowly, builds a bridge over it. She painfully describes the "groans" on both sides and the hope that awaits when we meet each other on that bridge.

On both sides there is isolation, fear, shame, and longing. I see it all the time. Young women trying to navigate the maze of their twenties and thirties, confused and disoriented. Women my age, navigating different decades with the same issues. We have so much to offer each other, but we so rarely come together.

Not long ago, I spent some time with a young woman in her twenties who had somewhat reluctantly asked if I would mind meeting her for coffee. As I listened, she unfolded relational, work, and personal issues that are so typical of the postcollege era. What was most remarkable to me was this: she was deeply comforted by my lack of shock over what she was experiencing. It was almost healing to her, she said, that I just listened, nodded, empathized, and then gave a few thoughts that might help.

I didn't need to give her answers; I didn't need to fix her or solve her problems. I needed to reassure her that nothing she was going through was out of the ordinary. I needed to reassure her that God was with her and that she was actually navigating some pretty tough stuff in really remarkable ways. She felt encouraged; I felt used by God.

There are *lots* of books out there—more than twelve million on Amazon.com at last count. This one is worth the read. We so desperately need the wisdom on these pages. And Pam, like any really good writer, pens from experience on both sides of the bridge. She offers hope. She reminds us of the power of a place—a place where we can go and be heard, not judged; be listened to and advised to be sure, but with love and grace. She offers, on that bridge, the restorative words "Me too."

If you're my age, which is over forty (by a bit!), you need this book. Put it on your bedside table and read a few pages every night. And when you've finished, ask God to prompt a few women who are under forty to whom you might offer that cup of coffee.

If you are under forty, you need this book. Put it on your bedside table and read a few pages every night. And when you've finished, ask God to give you the courage to approach a woman or two who you can see is "growing old well with God." Ask her to meet you for a cup of coffee. Ask her questions about her life, and tell her about yours.

And maybe, just maybe, if enough of us do this, the fabric of our very torn world will have a chance to heal.

Nancy Ortberg

Note from the Author

I have been working on this book on and off for seven years, but its message has been forming in me my entire adult life. I have spoken and written to hundreds about the topic of this book and have prayed through Scripture, asking God more questions than I can ever write about. Much of what I've discovered has been gained through relationships in my own life and those experienced by others. Some of these people are mentioned in this book (most names have been changed), and many of my experiences with them formed how I wrote what's in these pages. *A Friend in Me* is written for every believing woman who is a bit ahead in life from another woman. The work you hold in your hands is for your heart.

Every kind of Christian woman—conservative, moderate, liberal, suburbanite, city dweller, lover of liturgy, lover of charismatic worship, egalitarian, complementarian, single, or married—models and teaches something about God to the next generation. I have seen firsthand how difficult it has become for women across the generations to share deeply from their hearts, but I've got good news: I've also witnessed powerful transformations in women's hearts when we finally do. For more than fifteen years I've spoken with all kinds of women who love God and want to make a difference by bringing God glory through their ministries, jobs, and families. In my conversations and prayers with them, we always come back to the condition of their hearts—something that is holding them back from deeply loving the younger women in their lives. These seemingly negative ideas of themselves or the ways they are being perceived can hold them back from sharing their faith out loud.

I was there once too. For many years I did what many saw as "godly" work. I prayed, led retreats, met with younger women, and wrote Bible studies. I was always surprised and thankful when I was asked to minister, whether to twelve hundred people or to one person. However, during that time, I became overwhelmed by empathy for others and myself; I felt it was too much to bear. That's when God lured my heart to meditate on Psalm 119 for more than eighteen months. It's a psalm that gave me space to renew my thinking and heal my heart. God knew I was longing for something richer, deeper, fuller to counter the losses and disappointments I felt for myself and for others. As the poetic words from the psalm mirrored my own sufferings and doubts, God gave me what I really wanted: more of him. His Word became my safest place; his presence through his Word was closer to me than my own tumultuous emotions, circumstances, successes, or failures. I discovered that no emotion or thought was beyond his reach. After I spent months praying through the psalm and bowing my mind to the Spirit, God removed my heart of stone and gave me a singleness of heart that transformed my relationships and my service to him.

My prayer for you as you read this book is that you too will let God's steadfast love comfort you (Ps. 119:76).

Chapter One

A Young Woman's Longings

Tell me, what is it you plan to do with
your one wild and precious life?
Mary Oliver, "The Summer Day"

The driver of the dump truck saw the compact car head straight toward him. "Oh, God!" he screamed. "Let them see me."

Within seconds the two vehicles collided.

Shaking, the truck driver climbed down from his rig and rushed to the Ford Taurus. He reached in with his hand and saw a glimmer of life in the young driver. "Oh, Jesus."

The man responded with a moan.

"Do you want me to pray for you?" the truck driver asked. The young man—boy, really—squeezed his hand.

"Oh, Jesus" was all the truck driver could pray. And the young man was gone.

The truck driver would later report to the police, "When I looked over at the young woman, I knew she was dead."

It was 6:30 in the morning and the heat of that July day had not yet awakened. A desolate highway in rural Colorado was leading this young, newly engaged couple home from a week of visiting relatives. But they never made it. Anthony, twenty-four, had fallen asleep at the wheel an hour from home. Elisa, twenty-two, was killed instantly when the car slammed into the dump truck. Anthony was my husband's younger brother, and Elisa was Anthony's beloved.

The hours that followed were dark as Brad and I flew to Colorado to be with family. If grief has a sound, I heard it as I walked into my in-laws' home. It was late afternoon and all I heard was a moan coming from upstairs: "Anthony, Anthony, Anthony." It was a father longing for his son. Brad went to see his dad, then his mom, then his younger sister. As I worked up the courage to face his family, I wondered how we could ever fly back to our new home state, settle in, live life, and desire. I turned to face my husband of only three years; grief cloaked this once joy-filled and gregarious man.

For the next several months, I experienced the Father's compassion for the brokenhearted. Day after day, I turned toward Brad, no matter his response, and as I did, Jesus penetrated my inclination to run and hide. None of us were created to face or feel grief to its fullest capacity, and neither was Brad nor I. By God's grace I was able to create space so that we could grieve deeply together. But grief wasn't something I thought we would experience in our twenties. While the people around us accomplished their goals and made plans for their futures, Brad and I were drowning in pain.

The Lie That Says We Need Only Christ

The tragic deaths of my brother-in-law and his fiancée plunged me into unknown territory: Brad and I both experienced deep sadness over the loss of this incredible couple, and our sadness brought abrupt changes to our marriage. I could see the emptiness in Brad's life but was unable to navigate it. I felt helpless and overwhelmed as I watched my husband suffer. My female colleagues (I was an assistant professor of English at the time) assumed that since I was married, my need to open up was already being met. We lived thousands of miles away from our families of origin, so we were isolated in our grief. I was paralyzed emotionally and couldn't reach out for help. So my pursuit of Brad wasn't always healthy, because I wanted to make this tragic loss right, better, fixed.

Sitting at our small kitchen table with his head hung low, Brad would cry softly to himself. Conversation between us was forced. I cooked his favorite foods, called his buddies around the country to pray for him, and even walked unannounced into the academic dean's office where we worked and asked if someone at the college could please do something. I was demanding that God and others respond to our loss in a certain way. Why, I questioned, could no one, not even God, explain why this had happened to us?

I was giving but not receiving in those long days. And all the while I wondered why everyone around me thought I was so strong. I felt alone. Some girlfriends from my high school days drove two hours to our home to visit, and we had sweet times of tender sharing. But intermittent visits from close friends weren't enough. Looking back, I can see that what was missing was being able to talk daily about my pain and suffering and to hear about someone else's experience of suffering. Incapable of naming what my heart needed—to talk openly about my pain—I developed a skill of looking independent.

Several months into our grief, I heard God's voice. It happened as I was jogging. The running path wrapped itself around the community of townhouses where we lived and eventually unwrapped itself to several small ponds of water. I ran hard, hoping that when I returned home, Brad would be back to his usual self. But every day, for months, the scene, the sounds, the sights did not change.

Then one day I fell to my knees, overwhelmed by hopelessness and sadness for Brad, for his parents, for our marriage. I begged God to do something—to rescue Brad from this pain. In that moment with tears streaming down my face, I broke and confessed my demands of God, of others, and of myself. In the silence that followed, I heard these words: "Love him. Pam, love him. Love him, Pam." I had told God my desires. And God had told me his.

I remember thinking, *If only I had been reminded to do it sooner.* That's when the awareness came: I needed other women who had walked this path before to walk with me, or the suffering would take over and I would keep trying to fix Brad rather than love him.

We Need Others

The pain of losing Brad's brother and his fiancée brought me to an understanding: God wanted to fill the void that their deaths had created in my life and in Brad's. Any filling that could possibly satisfy such a void would come through closer relationships with friends, family, each other, and for me, other women.

I believe that God wants people close. Whether it is a man to his wife or a daughter to her mother or a friend to a friend, God created us for relationships. Closeness in the family is a demonstration of the Trinity, the love of God the Father, the bond with Jesus, and the fullness of the Holy Spirit.

All along, God wanted that closeness with me and for me with others; it was only as I peered into my lover's heart that stirrings for this relief were awakened. It was only through suffering and recognizing my need for healthy women to walk this road with me that stirrings for real healing began.

After that time on the running path, I began to accept that I should not ignore my longing for relief from pain and violent emotions. But I found it difficult to initiate the depth of conversation that I was longing for. At the time I didn't understand why it was so hard, but now I can see that I had a lot to lose. As a newly married woman, I didn't want to criticize or complain about my husband and risk someone judging him or our marriage. I was in my midtwenties, just getting established in my profession, and believed that if I shared with a colleague the waves of emotions I felt, she might question my capability to do my job. I was expected to lead and to lead well. I couldn't risk revealing my questions and doubts. Even more important, I couldn't find others who had similar chaotic feelings because I suspected people would question the depth of my faith in Christ if I shared my feelings with them. I didn't have a place to open up and tell the truth about what Brad and I were going through.

This tragic event exposed my longings and my needs, but because I didn't have deep relationships with other women, I was unable to get the help I needed to grieve well with the one I loved the most.

In the decades since, I've talked with hundreds of women who longed for friendships with women who were ahead of them in the seasons of life. I've come to believe that we have a problem, a crisis really: more and more women are feeling isolated from other women, especially between the generations. Unless we begin to respond to the need, I am convinced that this problem will only intensify given our rapidly changing culture. In Christian Smith's work *Lost in Transition*,[1] Smith and his collaborators interviewed more than two hundred emerging adults, investigating the difficulties young people face. The book identifies five major problems facing young Americans, even young Christians, today: confused moral reasoning, routine intoxication, materialistic life goals, regrettable sexual experiences, and disengagement from civic and political life. Could it be that by cultivating close relationships with the younger women in our lives we could help them navigate minefields like these? Smith seemed to think so. He claimed that much of the younger generation's pain and confusion lies with us, those who've gone before them.

What Younger Women Are Saying

The stories I have heard have convinced me that while the need for cross-generational friendships is great, many of us are sending negative messages that are keeping younger women at arm's length.

Karen is a thirty-two-year-old mom of two who works from home. She and her husband are committed Christians who started their marriage working in full-time ministry until their employer went under for financial fraud, causing the couple to seek other jobs.

Leery of organized Christian institutions, the couple stayed away from church involvement. Although they lived in the same city as their families, Karen rarely felt the support she needed from the more mature women in her life. This lack became only more obvious when she faced a crisis. She had started a home business, but it wasn't doing well, and she began to experience anxiety.

When she called her mom for help, Karen knew by her mother's response that she disagreed with some of the decisions Karen had made, especially her decision not to attend church. It felt to Karen as if her mom were withholding being close because of that one decision. By the tone of her voice and the questions her mom asked, Karen knew intuitively what her mom was thinking: *If you would have stayed in church, you wouldn't be in this mess.* Karen wasn't certain why she felt so anxious, but she was sure of one thing: she'd have to figure this out on her own. After her mom's continual suggestions of what to do—get more rest and talk to a counselor—Karen finally accepted that her mom couldn't do what she really needed: just be close to her and fully present. Karen was left feeling that she had to portray an image to her mom that her life was fine. She found temporary help through an online community, but the more she leaned on that community for direction, the more isolated she felt. When Karen's mom realized she was so involved with social media and still struggling with anxiety, she confronted her. Karen later said, "The sense I got from my mom is she wants to fix in my life what was wrong in hers."

Another friend, Amy, who is twenty-six years old, works as a program evaluation consultant for museums around the country. One day while we were having coffee, I asked her about her faith.

Tilting her head to one side and then the other, she said, "I love God. But I have a deep desire to be close to women ahead of me in the faith." She said that she had this kind of friendship when she was in college, but now that she works and is in the "real world," she feels ignored by women who are ahead of her in life. She's close to her mother and grandmother, but they live thousands of miles away. Amy told me that she'd been visiting a church in her area for close to four months and had never been approached or contacted by anyone from the church.

One Sunday she worked up the courage to talk to an older woman after the worship service. At one point during the conversation, the woman asked Amy what she did for work, and as she responded, the woman appeared distracted. Her body language communicated the message: *I am not interested in you.* "The shifting of her eyes gave her away. How could we build a meaningful friendship on that?" Amy said. She later confessed that she suspected the woman was intimidated by her because of the job she had. Amy just wanted to connect with another woman on a spiritual level, to talk about faith issues and her relationship with God. After that hurtful exchange she didn't want to shadow the door of church again. She told me, "I'm not doubting my faith; I'm longing for a closeness. It's exhausting depending on Facebook or email for connecting with others. I want something real."

Kate is another young woman who received negative messages when trying to reach out for help. She told me how one day she approached a woman in her office (a Christian nonprofit) to seek advice about living with her boyfriend. She wanted out of the arrangement but didn't know what steps to take. "I thought getting another woman's perspective would be the wise thing to do. My finances were complicated and I didn't make enough to live on my own." When she opened up about her dilemma, the woman told her, "Well, you got yourself into this mess; you better figure out how to move out."

When I asked what her mom thought, Kate said, "All my mom wants to know is when I'm planning to get married." Kate desperately wanted someone to go deeper with her, to talk through the details without judging her.

What Older Women Are Saying

After hearing stories like these from younger women, I was curious if women in their forties, fifties, and sixties were experiencing challenges getting close to the younger women in their lives. My answers came swiftly and in ways I hadn't anticipated.

When Brad and I were invited to teach a Sunday school class of about seventy-five fifty-year-olds, the couple in charge asked us to come and talk about our observations on the next generation. As we interacted with this group, I could see they knew Scripture well and considered church a priority. But what struck me was how many of the women voiced their longing for more of an intimate relationship with their adult children and grandchildren. One woman after another lamented the differences that kept their daughters, daughters-in-law, granddaughters, nieces, and younger-women friends at arm's length. Their comments and concerns revealed specific, even outrageous, expectations of what they wanted from their children and grandchildren, especially when it came to how they practiced their faith traditions. One woman stood in the back of the room and said, "Our daughter is not raising our grandchildren in the church the way we raised our children. How can we have a close relationship with her?" Another woman emailed me the next week and asked me to pray for her granddaughters because they were making lifestyle choices she didn't approve. "How can I show them the love of God when they are more interested in their boyfriends than in Christianity?" Clearly, these women recognized there was a problem, but they were oblivious to the solution. They are not alone in this.

Linda told me that after raising three sons on the family's fifty-acre tree farm, she was excited for much-needed girl time and was looking forward to being close to her daughters-in-law. Her sons had married within a few years of one another, and initially their wives had seemed eager to spend time together as a family. But Linda said the dynamics changed after the grandchildren came along. Somehow she found out that two of the families were planning a vacation together, but without her. The pain and sense of being left out were more than she could articulate. When she finally worked up the courage to ask why she hadn't been invited, one daughter-in-law said, "We needed time together as a family." The words were more painful than the action itself. When the wave of that incident finally blew over and she was on the phone with her oldest son's wife, Linda tried to explain how important it was to her that they be close, but her daughter-in-law's response had told Linda she didn't trust her. Linda was at a loss as to why. She later told a friend, "I long to have an intimacy with my own daughters-in-law that they just don't need from me. I can't even ask them about church. Why can't we be close?"

The Problem: Distancing Messages

Many of the messages we send, intentional or not, are hurting our relationships with the younger women in our families, churches, neighborhoods, and workplaces. When we shift our eyes, square our shoulders, or stand a bit away in conversation, we are sending a message that says, *Something you said or something about you is wrong.* Many times our words, our responses, and our body language say, *I am unsafe.*

Without someone to talk openly with about deeper spiritual issues, sexuality, and practical daily living, younger women feel a sense of isolation. They long for someone a little ahead of them in life to walk closely with them. Yet, across the board, younger women are saying older women don't initiate or follow up when they offer an opportunity for us to be involved with their lives.

What I hear the younger generation asking for is this: for us to be more aware of the way we live our lives in front of them. What tone of voice do we take when talking with the younger women in our lives? What are we thinking when a younger woman tells us about a serious problem? Do we take the time to linger in her presence? Are we willing to go deep with awkward conversations? Can we listen to a young woman express her doubts, anxiety, or depression and resist the urge to fix her? Have we figured out how to be honest about our own journeys without wanting her to be just like us? What repels a younger woman further from us is when she cannot connect her own doubts and struggles with our surface talk. Being real about our doubts and struggles draws her to us. It sends her the message *You have a friend in me.*

Does It Really Make a Difference?

In 2012, I interviewed and met with younger Christian women ages nineteen to forty. The question burning inside me was, do younger women need older women to grow spiritually? Hands down, the answer was a resounding yes. Not only did the women say yes, but the tone of their voices changed and they lowered their eyes to hide the tears.

Many of the younger women in your life are hungry to share with you what they believe God is saying to them—even if you don't agree with their conclusions. They want your openness, vulnerability, and availability.

As I sat listening to each of these young women, I recognized their longing—the longing to be in the presence of someone who has experienced a similar brokenness. I recognized my own longing twenty years earlier as a young married woman. I remembered the spiritual exhaustion and feeling unsafe. I put my pen down, looked around the room, and wondered what it would take for the older generation to become a safe place and heal this divide.

Closeness Is Possible

I am convinced that young women in the church are longing for help in understanding spiritual things, especially how they relate their faith to their everyday lives. They want to make a greater commitment to knowing God and Scripture. But they require more of us in relationship so that they can understand how their faith influences all areas of their lives.

I wrote this book in order to help Christian women learn how to intentionally stay in relationship with the women closest to them—how to initiate, sustain, strengthen, and spend time with the younger women they love and come in contact with on a regular basis.

I believe we are living in an unusual time. It's unlike the past when we could depend on organized religion and institutions to pass our faith to the next generation. As I have taught and spoken in different parts of the country, I have observed how the median age at women's retreats and conferences is well over forty, leaving me to wonder where the younger generation is going for spiritual support.

If we are willing to forget the past and make a wholehearted commitment to move forward, we can transform the messages we are sending. If we fail to change the way we are relating, we will gamble away an opportunity to demonstrate Christ's extraordinary love to the next generation. The women closest to us will continue to believe we are judging them and trying to fix them and make them just like us. It may not be true, but they will likely continue to feel this way.

So, in the first part of this book, we're going to explore what we can do to become vulnerable, available, and safe in our relationships. We will find out what we need from Christ and how to put it into practice so we can become safe havens for others. We'll spend a couple of chapters exploring how to talk with younger women about sex, friendships, and work.

Do not be overwhelmed. God, through the power of the Holy Spirit, is already at work on this issue. There is at least one younger woman in your life who longs for you to come alongside her, to help her negotiate and navigate the chaos of her feelings and the shifting ground of the changing world. As you read through these chapters,

I'm inviting you to look for the truth not only inside yourself but also outside yourself so that you can invest your life in the women behind you.

The church can be a place where women can once again be themselves. Leaders can help women hear there's a better way to live than what culture and media offer. The church can encourage women to pattern their lives in such a way that others can "stand at the crossroads and look; ask for the ancient paths, ask where the good way is, and walk in it" (Jer. 6:16). One woman's life can lead another woman to find rest for her soul. Like Mary Oliver, I want to know, what is it you plan to do with your one wild and precious life?

Chapter Two

Safe Havens

When we were children, we used to think that when we were
grown-up we would no longer be vulnerable. But to grow up
is to accept vulnerability.... To be alive is to be vulnerable.

Madeleine L'Engle, *Walking on Water*

When I was in high school, my language arts teacher was Ms. Andraka. Michelle, as I later called her, was twenty-seven, single, and living in Center City, Philadelphia. She seemed happy and had a knack for asking students good questions.

It was known around school that Michelle talked a lot about the Bible and God and Campus Crusade. I'd grown up going to church and enjoyed prayer, even as a teenager, but I didn't think talking about my relationship *with* God *with* my teacher was cool, even though I went to a Christian high school. Even so, Michelle and I developed a relationship inside and outside the classroom.

High school is nothing I would want to repeat. In fact, I made enough poor choices to warrant myself the talk of my church. It's not easy for a young girl with a daring personality and lots of passions to listen to sermons on sin and the holiness of God. But the truth is, I had a genuine interest in spiritual things. My problem, however, was that I also had a genuine interest in good times and hot guys. So for a few years, I pursued all of my passions. When you are in high school, you have it in the back of your mind that "one day" you will stop doing what you're not supposed to do. That can be translated as "One day I will stop living with all kinds of desires."

At the beginning of my junior year, I knew I wanted to attend college, so I broke up with my boyfriend who was much older than I was and started to dream about a career. It was about that time that Michelle and I started having deeper conversations. She was the one person who knew about both my lives. Talking openly with Michelle seemed natural; I never remember her pulling away from me, shifting her eyes, or thinking she wanted to fix me. One day, when we were enjoying appetizers at a restaurant in downtown Philadelphia, she asked me about my relationship with Jesus.

"It's great!" I said. "Jesus is really cool. But I don't really fit with what it means to be a Christian girl—I'm nothing like the others."

Michelle laughed loud enough for the other patrons to look over at us. "Pam! I love that you're so transparent. Of course you're not like other Christians—you're not supposed to be. Jesus is pursuing you for his purposes, not yours or theirs."

Something about Michelle's response was freeing. She didn't lecture me on the way I dressed or the friends I hung out with at school. She didn't make me feel like I was this rebellious teenager about to ruin my future. She didn't assume that I knew who God was just because I went to church and attended a religious high school. She was determined, humble, and flexible in meeting me exactly where I was and as I was, without trying to change me. She gave me space to talk about the longings in my heart, the good longings and the bad. I could tell she wasn't about religion but about something spiritual.

Despite our age difference, I felt free to open up with Michelle. Through the end of my senior year of high school, we met often. She was a safe haven for me, more than any woman I had in my life up to that point.

Jesus, Our Example

We live in a media-saturated world where women of all ages seem more connected than ever before. Our problem is we outwardly appear to be close to other women when in fact women feel more isolated than ever. Consequently, many young women want mentors, guides, and role models to whom they can bring their accomplishments and failures to feel affirmed, mutually respected, and understood.

Jesus is a brilliant example of what it means to be a safe haven for others. When we examine his relationship with his disciples, we see that he allowed them to be themselves, even if that meant they would resist his ideas. According to John, who devoted eight chapters of his book to the last hours of Jesus's life, in the weeks up to his death, Jesus didn't minister to the crowds; instead, he spent time with his closest friends (John 13:1–30). The gospel writer was showing how much Jesus prioritized personal relationships.

Since Jesus knew the reason God had sent him to earth in the first place and was aware of his season of life, I think we can assume that every word he said and every act he performed had purpose. He was determined to serve his disciples.

Eagerly desiring to show his closest friends something more, Jesus did something for them that, as far as we know, he never did for other human beings: he knelt and washed the feet of all twelve of his disciples. When he came to Peter and lowered himself, Peter objected. He insisted that this Messiah, Lord, and Savior could not wash his dirty feet. On the surface it might have seemed as though Peter was being humble, but that wasn't the case. His words betrayed his self-reliance: "You shall never wash my feet" (John 13:8). He had no real desire to do Christ's will. Jesus wisely saw the bigger picture and didn't walk away from or ignore his friend. Nor did he criticize him for his outburst. Instead, he loved him without condition, giving Peter the freedom to express whatever was on his mind.

When people feel safe, they often reveal their truest natures. As Christ revealed his own humility by lowering himself to wash the disciples' feet, Peter revealed his spiritual independence. Jesus responded, "Unless I wash you, you have no part with me." I imagine Jesus's tone of voice here was one of disappointment, not condemnation. Peter then tried to instruct Jesus to wash his hands and head as well. Still Jesus didn't react with condemnation or impatience, making Peter feel even safer.

When Jesus healed the sick, the disciples saw his compassion; when he cast out demons and fed the five thousand, they saw his supernatural power. But in this scene, they saw his nature: open and humble. After he washed the disciples' feet, Jesus told them to do this for one another and to expect a blessing.

There is a lesson here for those of us who want to build bridges to the next generation: *when we are humble, others are free to be open around us.*

Qualities of Safe Havens

Is the core of your heart a safe place? Can you give others the space to grow, fail, and mature?

David Kinnaman, author of *You Lost Me*, said, "To follow Jesus, young adults in the next generation—just like the generations before them—will have to learn humility. From whom will they learn it? When they look at us, do they see humble servants and eager students of the Master?"[1] Jo Saxton, author of *Influential*, said that to reach the next generation we must be accessible and transparent.

The qualities of a safe haven are as follows.

Humble

Our ability to serve those around us depends largely on why we're doing the serving. The humbler we are—the more aware we are of God's working power in our lives—the more we can get up from the table, so to speak, set aside what others may think, and give to those closest to us. We can confidently lay aside anything that would get in the way of loving. When our determination to serve equals what God has given us, other women begin to open up their hearts to us. They find us to be shelters in whom they can relax and feel accepted.

When we are humble, we are rarely threatened or embarrassed or insecure. (If we become aware that we are struggling with feeling threatened or insecure, we acknowledge it but don't let it hold us back.) We are free to focus on the other person and to be present to her.

When we are humble, it paves the way for "oneness." In John 17:11, Jesus prayed to his Father, asking him to keep his followers in his name, "that they may be one as we are one." Oneness is a connection that happens right now. People are spiritually formed when we are forming together in that present moment. With age, we can forget how to be "one" with a younger woman—meaning we forget how to be her friend. Yet being one with another person is basically finding ways to agree with that person. We are one with a younger woman when we find ways to identify with her: "How's the child care coming along? I remember when I first started working after my baby was born." Or "I'm not feeling motivated to exercise. How do you discipline yourself so well?" When we are one with a younger woman, we give her a model for what her relationship with Christ could look like: authentic, safe, practical, intimate, and conversational. When we humbly admit that we want to learn how to support her by being ourselves, we help her experience her identity in Christ. We help her understand what it means to be loved and to be worthy. We help her recognize that her relationship with Christ can be accessible and transparent.

We also help her understand her dependency on Christ by the way we talk about our lives, our ministries, our families, our jobs, or our "brands." Many of us don't realize that we can often sound as though we do things on our own. Yet consider Christ's relationship to his Father. In John 8:28, he said, "I do nothing on my own but speak just what the Father has taught me." When a younger woman leaves your presence, would she say the same about you? The next conversation you have with her may be the only time she hears "I'm learning to listen more and more to the Spirit, and I only do what he tells me." When your words and actions reveal your dependence on him and everything he has done for you, you help the young women in your life to understand that they too must be dependent on him.

However, if you have self-reliance at the center of your relationship with Jesus, that's what you will pass along to others; it's spiritually impossible not to do so.

Committed to the Relationship

I've experienced a wide variety of relationships with women through work, church, ministry, neighborhoods, and friendships over the years. Not one of those relationships was without its problems. One or two women left the relationship out of offense. Others insisted on being the center of attention. Close relationships can come and go; the strong ones will stay, and we gladly benefit from them. Even when a relationship has problems, it can be one in which "iron sharpens iron" (Prov. 27:17). Properly navigated, close relationships can give a woman such a strong sense of belonging, and the love and support she receives will far outweigh the bad.

Able to Invite Others to Be Vulnerable

When we invite younger women to share their deeper feelings with us, they feel our love for them. When my friend Olivia slipped in next to me in church one Sunday, I could tell immediately she was trying to hide that something was bothering her. I knew I could just let her be or I could invite her to tell me what was going on in her heart. I leaned over and asked if she was okay. She held herself back and smiled, saying she would be all right. I've known Olivia for several years; our husbands work together and she and I minister together, and I knew she didn't want to burden me. She had fallen into self-reliance, so I persisted, "I can tell something's wrong." Then I told her how much I loved her. I'm just enough ahead of her in life to feel confident around my or others' chaotic feelings. They don't intimidate me anymore. And I've experienced God's peace in those places when someone else spoke a word of truth to me. So I "got up from the table and knelt" before her. Then I said, "If you can't tell me the truth, we can't be close friends." With that, her tears started, and after church she opened up to me. I cried with her so she could say what she needed to say.

It's important that we send a message to the younger women in our lives that says, "I love you, but you need to be real with me." In this way, we create an environment where women are free to open up emotionally. How else can we expect to speak the truth into someone's life?

Becoming a Safe Haven

If as you are reading this you are wondering whether you are a safe haven, here are some things to consider.

Pay Attention to Your Tone of Voice

My fifteen-year-old daughter has made it her mission to remind me of the tone of my voice when I'm interacting with our family. Her friendly reminders usually happen when I'm multitasking, because I'm horrible at it, and my voice changes tones when I'm frustrated. "Girls! Whose turn is it to unload the dishwasher?" Suddenly, I hear a sweet voice behind me say, "Mom, try it this way." (Imagine a soft, sweet, lighthearted tone.) "Giiirls, whose turn is it to unload the dishwasher?" We all laugh at this, but she's right. Our tone of voice can make all the difference when it comes to whether we are sending a message that says, "You can talk to me about anything and you won't be judged or criticized or confronted."

One young friend told me, "The second I hear my mom's voice on the phone, the tone of her voice tells me if we are going to have a good conversation or not."

A student once said this about a woman professor: "Her tone was so accusing when I asked her questions in class." Later when I mentioned this to the professor in confidence, she shook her head and said, "I was just trying to move on to my lecture." I was saddened by this response because the professor clearly had missed the point.

The pace of our lives authorizes the tones of our voices more than we realize. As Carl Jung often said, "Hurry isn't of the devil; it is the devil."[2]

There are a number of ways to remind ourselves about this. I recommend that women ask others for feedback about their tones of voice. It's a good way to show you are vulnerable and open to suggestions. You can also stand in front of a mirror and watch yourself as you speak on the phone. You can see what you look like when you use a particular tone. It can also help to take five seconds to breathe deeply before every interaction.

Renew Your Thinking

Alayna, an eighth grader who is a good student and active in sports, was the recipient of an unhealthy sexting and emailing relationship with a boy from her class. When her parents found out and everyone involved gathered for a meeting, Alayna hung her head in shame, not wanting to make eye contact with the adults who expected so much of her. As the meeting began, the school nurse made eye contact with her and said, "Before anything else is said to you, I want you to know that wondering about sex is a normal teenaged thing. There's nothing wrong with you for being curious. It's normal for you to be flattered by a boy's attention." With those compassionate words, this wise woman helped Alayna drop her guard and be willing to receive proper training from the adult women in her life.

When younger women tell you things that are painful and possibly even shameful for them, what thoughts go through your mind? Are you shocked? Judgmental? Critical? Put off? Or are you compassionate and loving?

To become more compassionate, caring, and safe, you may have to renew your thinking. The younger generation needs to hear us using good sense with them when they talk with us about serious situations in their lives. They need to see that we are open-minded, not set in our natural way of seeing things. If we are living in a way that pleases God, we renew our minds by the power of the Holy Spirit, who enables us to see things anew, not from our natural perspective.

When I think of women who renew their thinking through the power of the Holy Spirit and who shelter others in their presence, I think of Dana, who applies what she's studying in Scripture to her own life first. Because her inward thoughts are meditating on Scripture, the first words out of her mouth are good and helpful.

For instance, after Laura eloped with a young man her parents disapproved of, her family cut off all communication with her. When

Dana started meeting with her, the first thing she said to her was "Laura, what's done is done. If you need to confess anything you did wrong to God or your parents, do it. Otherwise, you need to get back to the business of living life." She didn't ask, "Why did you do such a foolish thing?" Nor did she criticize her parents.

You can renew your thinking in dozens of ways. For example, broaden your perspective by reading books by different authors, even ones you might disagree with. Pursue relationships with women who differ from you theologically and educationally. Renew your perspective by listening first in a situation. Withholding your opinion is a way of considering someone's need more important than your own. As you wait to speak, you may become aware of how you stereotype others and their situations, thinking things such as *That sounds like something a liberal person would say* or *That sounds like something an evangelical would do.*

Women who take active steps to renew their minds have a much greater chance of becoming safe havens.

Take the Time

Adrienne, who is an administrator in a hospital, set aside a few hours on a Saturday afternoon to cook with a group of twentysomething women she had met through a gathering. She had asked them what they would like to do together, and these single professionals said they wanted to learn to cook new recipes and talk about spiritual issues.

Another woman I know takes special trips with each of her granddaughters. She chooses a week out of the year to spend with each one. She plans the trip, buys the tickets, and reserves that time just for the two of them. They eat out, visit museums, and see shows. She even took one of her granddaughters on a hot air balloon ride. On returning from one of these trips, she said to me, "My heart is full." I'm happy for this woman, because I know how often her daughters, granddaughters, and nieces initiate contact with her. I'm convinced that the amount of time she takes to linger in their presence demonstrates to these young women that she hears and loves them.

Other women I know take the time to connect regularly with the younger women they care about via scheduled Skype or FaceTime calls. When relatives or family friends do this, my daughters look forward to the call if it's scheduled in advance. As Annie Dillard said about time, "A schedule defends from chaos and whim. It is a net for catching days. It is a scaffolding on which a worker can stand and labor with both hands at sections of time."[3]

Avoid Fragmentation and Superficiality

The enemy wants our most intimate thoughts for himself, so he tries to keep women from being close to one another. I believe he uses two things to thwart closeness and to keep us from being safe havens for one another: fragmentation and superficiality.

1. Fragmentation. We give away little pieces of ourselves all day long. Our minds are always on the next thing or on what we just finished, keeping us from focusing on what is in front of us.

When our lives are fragmented, we often lose our sense of joy and our sense of purpose. That's the case for a pastor friend who shared with me how her greatest regret in the last decade is being too busy. "I don't regret pursuing my job, but I regret the busyness, and I don't know how to stop." Even though she wants to be close to the women in her life, she's starting to recognize that busyness is sending the opposite message to others: *Don't pursue me or you might just take more from me.* When our lives are busy and fragmented, we can't shelter others with our presence. We keep people standing on the perimeter of our lives, fearful that if they break one more piece off us, our entire worlds will shatter.

When I'm fragmented, I resist spending one-on-one and face-to-face time with people. I withdraw, hoping I can regroup on my own. The antidote to fragmentation is opening up and having deep conversations in the midst of feeling chaotic.

When my daughters announce that they are going to try a new sport or join another club or youth group, I often talk with them about what would happen if they were to say yes to everything. They would feel frazzled and tired, not to mention that I couldn't possibly drive them everywhere they would want to be! With each new opportunity, we decide together if saying yes to something will cause one of our lives to become fragmented. I want my girls to know that life-giving conversations with them matter to me and I don't want to sacrifice those important talks.

When asked to do something for someone, these are good questions to ask yourself: Do I want to say yes out of greed? Am I afraid of missing out on what others have?

Busyness isn't the only thing that leads to fragmentation—so do neglecting God's purposes, not recognizing where you are in God's timetable, forgetting what God has given you, and not spending enough time having life-giving conversations with the women closest to you. Deeper conversations remind us about our true purpose and the unique strengths God has given us and, therefore, satisfy any desires we may have for wanting more than we already have.

2. Superficiality. Superficiality is relating to only the surface. It's a concern with only the obvious or the apparent, not the profound or thorough; it implies a lack of depth. It is a neglect of details through haste or indifference. One author described some in the American church as superficial by saying that they are "a mile wide and an inch deep."[4]

Social media doesn't mitigate this culture of superficiality. For example, we can post photos where we look our best or delete comments we don't like. Nor is social media a safe place where women can share and be vulnerable. In fact, studies show women who have a prolonged usage of Facebook are more affected than men when it comes to their self-esteem.[5] One friend who recently lost a loved one told me she doesn't understand why women will write thoughtful messages on her Facebook page but never talk about her loss when she sees them in person. "What's wrong with asking me to my face how I'm doing and waiting for me to answer? I get the impression most women don't want to hear what I might say."

To initiate deeper conversations with women, start remembering details they tell you or post online and ask them specific questions the next time you are together. Ask about personal things, but also ask about their work and skills and how Jesus is leading them. Ask what they believe their strengths are. What are the skills God equipped them with, and how do those skills impact their present or future work?

Recently, I posed that question to a small group of twenty-four-year-old women, and each one said she hadn't thought about it before. Our conversation went beyond the surface as we stayed on that topic for more than an hour. It was satisfying to stay focused, to go deeper, and hear them think aloud about how their God-given skills are helping them to discover their work and, ultimately, who they are.

Embrace These Five Life-Giving Patterns

I am convinced we can become more like Christ and influence the next generation, but in order to do so, we must first receive and embrace five life-giving patterns that are found in Psalm 119:73–80:

> Your hands made me and formed me;
> give me **understanding** to learn your commands.
> May those who fear you rejoice when they see me,
> for I have put my hope in your word.
> I know, O LORD, that your laws are righteous,
> and in faithfulness you have **afflicted** me.
> May your **unfailing** love be my comfort,
> according to your promise to your servant.
> Let your **compassion** come to me that I may live,
> for your law is my delight.
> May the arrogant be put to shame for
> wronging me without cause;
> but I will meditate on your precepts.
> May those who fear you turn to me,
> those who understand your statutes.
> May my heart be **blameless** toward your decrees,
> that I may not be put to shame.[6]

The five patterns are as follows: learning to deal with suffering, giving healing comfort, acting with understanding, knowing full forgiveness, and relating with compassion. Like a solitary diamond flanked by five smaller ones on a ring, God's steadfast love is set in the center of these patterns. Can we practice them until they become the very fabric of our being? I think we can, as long as we accept that we won't be perfect. I'm so thankful I said yes to this journey, as the patterns have not only transformed my relationships but also healed my heart in the process.

Jesus personified these patterns that day when he washed his disciples' feet. When we live out these patterns, we, as he did, will make relationships a priority. Will you join me in seeking to become a safe haven so that we can be an extension of the church for this next generation?

Jesus was able to sit at a table with both his beloved and his betrayer because he knew where he came from and where he was going. As the Son of God, he knew his purpose in suffering; he was determined to comfort the ones he loved and to show compassion to those who hurt. He understood that his disciples related to him and one another out of pride, which resulted in a competitive spirit, and he knew we would struggle with that too. Take some time and pay attention to the women around you. Don't you sense that women are longing to stay connected and to have more satisfying relationships? I believe we can't meet those needs in our flesh. We need these patterns to show our best love, the full extent of a divine love.

Chapter Three

The Other Side of Pain and Suffering

*By denying their pain, avoiding the necessary falling, many
have kept themselves from their own spiritual depths—and
therefore have been kept from their own spiritual heights.*

Richard Rohr, *Falling Upward*

A few years ago, I traveled to Mount Saint Helens with fifty middle
schoolers, teachers, and parents. I don't camp; I'm high maintenance
about food, sleeping, and, well, just about everything. When the Ape
Cave excursion was first mentioned, the word *hike* was used. Hiking
is good; it's not camping. On the morning of the excursion, a morning after sleeping in old wooden cabins without heat, we drove to
Cougar, Washington, lined up at the cave entrance, walked inside,
and stepped down. I remember wondering where the experts were.
Not a single establishment or park ranger could be seen for miles. As
we continued down into the center of the earth, I felt well equipped

with my warm coat and headlamp. But no one could have prepared me for what happened during the next three hours. Aside from the narrow beams from our tiny headlamps, we walked in complete darkness, our hands groping along the walls so we could find our way.

When the groups behind and in front separated from us, the dark became darker. I hadn't noticed before how black comes in shades. The sound of silence made me lose my sense of direction. At that moment I faced a dreadful feeling of fear unlike any I have ever known. I could feel panic's hands around my neck. With three young girls near me, I knew I had to take the responsibility to lead us out. Petrified, all my spirit could utter was *Show me one light. Just one light. God, please, show me one light.* Crawling on our stomachs through the caves, we could not see inches in front of us. We moved forward with a mixture of fear and faith along the dark, cold rock. Finally, we saw the lights ahead. Winding through the caves for another hour, I drank in darkness while fear still shook in my blood. When we caught up with our group, my relief was palpable.

That affliction, that fear, was not something I wanted in my life. Yet it commanded my attention. I was so focused on getting out of the situation that I was able to let go of what was unimportant and focus solely on the two things I needed to do at that moment: find the lights and support those closest to me.

Getting to the Gold

We are living in a time when we can be easily deceived.[1] In part, we are easily deceived because we are so isolated from one another, especially from other generations. Overall, we lack a regard and respect for our teachers, pastors, and leaders. We're also deceived because we've been seduced into thinking we don't need spiritual guidance or instruction. We have a wrong perspective of Scripture, or we assume we know what it's saying. I've heard some Christian women question God's Word as an authority in their lives. When they are suffering and need a light to lead them out, these young women have nothing brighter to focus on than their own pain; this leads to hopelessness. Yet Scripture says we have hope in the midst of suffering, and part of our job is to share the hope we have with the next generation.

Keep in mind that the information younger women need from us is not more intellectual knowledge. What they need from us is our stories—both the sad parts and the happy parts, our missteps and failures and our right steps and successes. And they need to hear about our pain and suffering, perhaps most of all. One of the young women I interviewed said, "I feel a distance from older women of faith because I rarely see a transparency and honesty that connects to my own doubts and struggles. Don't older women realize that when they are real about their suffering, it helps me with my second-guessing?" What this young woman was saying was that she longed for women who would share with her the spiritual wisdom and understanding they had gained on the other side of suffering.[2]

In our fallen world, the question is not whether we will experience suffering. The questions are when and how we will respond to suffering when it comes. Before we face pain and suffering, we often believe the world and our comforts revolve around us. We see everything that happens to us through our selfish perspectives because we haven't yet been refined by God's process. It's paramount for our spiritual growth that we get to the other side of suffering—that's where we find the gold. It's the gold we pass along to the next generation.

Jesus knew his purpose on this earth was to glorify God with the power given him. As Christian women, we must have that same perspective, but our lives can bring glory to him from only one position: an absolute willingness to be taught and helped. A life possessed by God in the face of suffering is a life worth living. Self-pity, which is essentially turning inward in suffering, brings forth more of the same and takes others down with it. There's only one way to get to the other side of suffering and to find the gold of spiritual wisdom and understanding. It's to do what God wants you to do. We get closer to the other side of the pain the more we let God come in and do what he wants to do.

That's what King Josiah did.

An Old Testament Model

Josiah's story is revealed in the Old Testament. He was an ideal king who reigned in Judah, a king who was prophesied about more than two hundred years earlier (1 Kings 13). The Scriptures say that King Josiah surpassed King David in his faithfulness to God (2 Kings 22). Early in his reign, Josiah launched a massive effort to abolish pagan worship throughout Israel and Judah. He made it his aim to repair the temple of the Lord.

Most likely Josiah heard stories about what God expected of his people, but at this time, there was no copy of the Holy Scriptures in anyone's hands. Josiah had never heard God's expectations of a king because the book of the law[3] had been lost for more than four hundred years. Somewhere along the way, the book of the law was either carelessly tossed to the side or maliciously hidden by an idolatrous king. Whatever happened, someone didn't want it to see the light of day. Then one day some workers in the temple uncovered the sacred writings.

The secretary told King Josiah, "We were paying our workmen for taking care of the temple when the high priest gave me a book, and I want to read it to you." When Josiah heard the words of the book and what God expected of him and his people, he tore his clothes because he was so upset. Josiah was devastated because he saw how God was dishonored, and he heard the ruin that was about to come to his people. Recognizing the holy words of God, he ordered his officials to find out what was going on and to pray to God (2 Kings 22:1–21).

Instead of trying to control the situation, instead of letting the pain and anxiety settle too long in his blood, instead of regretting the past four hundred years, Josiah humbled himself and cried out to God. "I'm seeking you. I'm asking you. I am so broken before you that I want you to seek me too. Search me; I give you full permission to search me." In essence, Josiah's heart was tender—tender enough that he could be taught and helped by God. In asking God to search him, he was asking God to show him if there was any sin in his heart. Was there something he could do right here and now that God wanted him to focus on? Josiah was asking for more of God—his plans, his thoughts, his perspective. More important than the pain he felt was the deep need to obey God's commands; so instead of fixating on his pain, he focused on what God had to say.

Josiah willingly dealt with his suffering in the presence of Someone who knew his heart better than he did. Absolute surrender was the only way to get to the other side of his suffering.

Like me, Josiah was in a dark cave, unable to see a way out. But he embraced the pain, and as he did, he humbled himself before God, surrendering all he had previously thought a godly king should be. He was now learning the fear of the Lord.

What can we learn from Josiah about how we should respond when suffering comes into our lives?

Humble Yourself before God

When Scripture tells us that Josiah "tore his robes," it means he literally tore his outer garments as a sign of his repentance and grief. It was customary at this time in Jewish history for loud cries and wailing to be heard when a person was broken before God. Similarly, when we cry out to God, we are asking for his presence to come even closer, because the pain and suffering are too much. We humble ourselves because we need God's help to take the next step.

Josiah's heart was remorseful, even though he had not been aware that he and his people had been sinning. When our suffering is caused by sinful or unwise choices that we've made—and even when it is caused by another's sin toward us—we too must fling ourselves onto the sovereignty of God. It's an act of humility because it is an acknowledgment of our insufficiency and his sufficiency.

I saw this kind of humility modeled a few years ago when a family from our girls' school lost their home and pets in a fire. They were devastated by such instant loss of past and present. Later when

I visited with the dad, he said, "In that moment, our only thought was *Everything belongs to God*."

When God saw Josiah's broken spirit, he said, "Because your heart was responsive and you humbled yourself ... I also have heard you.... Your eyes will not see all the disaster I am going to bring" (2 Kings 22:19–20). This is so important for us to grasp: when we surrender and bring our broken selves into the presence of God, we are so focused we become more aware of his presence than at any other time in our lives (Ps. 34:18). His nearness is palpable. When our response to pain and suffering is humility, we give God the freedom to liberate us from ourselves and from others so he can do a mighty work.

Plead with Others to Pray

Josiah received this gift of pain that was his alone. But like Jesus in the garden of Gethsemane, when Josiah was overwhelmed with sorrow, he asked those closest to him to keep watch and pray (Matt. 26:38).

Pain sears us. It can hollow us too. I know that when affliction comes upon me and I let it settle too long in my bones and blood, I relate to those closest to me in fear. I turn inward and focus on self-pity instead of on God's purposes for the suffering. When I don't ask God to search my inner spirit, suffering can turn me into a bitter, cynical, controlling woman. If I let that happen, I will be in an even worse place of pain than I already am.

Because it is so personal, suffering can tempt us to isolate ourselves. But when we cut ourselves off from others, especially the women in our lives, we are exactly where the enemy wants us. We must fight the urge to separate ourselves from others for too long. If we are to become safe havens for others in our lives, we must be willing to humble ourselves in the presence of God and ask those closest to us to seek the face of God for us.

That's what Jesus did. I'm so thankful for his example in the garden of Gethsemane. He prayed to the Father because he knew his suffering wasn't meaningless. He wanted his friends, the disciples, to fight alongside him in prayer. He didn't deny the agony of his suffering. He was brutally honest in his cries to God and begged God to take the cup of suffering from him. But because of his deep love for us, he said, "Yet not as I will, but as you will" (Matt. 26:39).

That's exactly what we must do. We must plead with others to pray for us and with us. We pray on our own for those we love and who love us. We cry out for wisdom, knowing God will respond.

Our suffering and our lives are never wasted when they are surrendered to God, because along the way he gives us pieces of gold that we can share with others. But the process of getting to the other side—to wisdom's gold—takes both our own prayers and the prayers of others.

Plead with God to Search Your Heart

King Josiah begged God to search his heart by tearing his clothes *and* sending his officials to pray to the Lord (2 Kings 22:11–13). Recognizing that only God knew what was truly happening, Josiah set an emergency team in motion to search for whatever would block God from getting involved and acting quickly.

Why did he want God to search his heart? For one thing, he wanted God's favor. While Josiah hadn't sinned deliberately against God, he realized God's Word wasn't being followed or implemented in any way. By pleading with God to search his heart, he was asking God to reveal anything that would hinder God's favor or keep him from following God's commands any longer.

When we go through suffering, we may be tempted to think, *I've done something wrong and that's why I'm suffering. God is punishing me.* That's rarely the case. So we need to ask God what's at the source of our suffering. If we are suffering due to no fault of our own, we still must ask God to search our hearts for anything that is blocking what he wants to do. Are we teachable? Are we willing for God to help us?

We ask God to search us so we can discover the truth and transcend our circumstances in order for our lives to have more of God's Spirit and less of our flesh. Even though Josiah knew the truth in part, he still needed God to search him to ensure his own thoughts and feelings wouldn't get in the way of God's purposes. We need to do the same. Like the psalmist, we must cry out, "Search me, God, and know my heart; test me and know my anxious thoughts. See if there is any offensive way in me, and lead me in the way everlasting" (Ps. 139:23–24).

The Hebrew word for "inquire of" in 2 Kings 22:13 is *daras*. It means "to seek, to consult, to ponder," and it also means "to be sought after, to let oneself be inquired, to allow a search to be made." King Josiah pleaded with God to search him, and because he wanted a full picture, he asked others to seek God on his behalf too. His officials called on Huldah the prophetess for prayer, and she was so in tune with God that Josiah found out immediately what was on God's heart and mind.

When the focus of our attention becomes all about hearing from God, we find the most resourceful people we know. Josiah's focus was clear: to find out what God was trying to tell him. Perhaps the purpose of God searching our hearts is to bring everything that's in them out to the open.

God helped Kimberly sift through her pain when her doctor told her she would never have children of her own. For the first few days, the finality of the doctor's words, "You are infertile," clung to her as she wept on her bathroom floor. She knelt on the cold floor and begged God to help her deal with the pain. Then she sent an SOS text to a friend that said, "I'm a mess. Dr. declared me infertile." Less than thirty minutes later, her friend sat by her on the floor and cried with her. As her friend cried out to God for her, she said, "God, search Kimberly's heart as this reality takes root and show her the new path you have for her."

Years later, as Kimberly served on a church staff as a spiritual director, she shared with a group of women how God lovingly had used her worst nightmare to give her hundreds of spiritual children. "He answered me when I called out to him. And sometimes it wasn't pretty. But the way God answered me has changed the way I viewed not having biological children." Kimberly was able to tell others about her deep sadness and what God did with it only because she humbled herself to God's searching of her in the deepest places. In so doing, she heard that her value and fulfillment were not attached to giving birth. She also saw how she was free to invest herself in others differently from most women she knew. If we, like Josiah and

Kimberly, will humble ourselves in the presence of God, plead with others to pray for us, and beg God to search us in the deeper parts, our suffering can lead to spiritual wisdom and understanding.

What Scripture Says about Suffering

Some segments of our Christian culture disagree with what I am saying and are still trying to persuade us to avoid pain and to seek prosperity and personal fulfillment. Yet true Christian teaching from Scripture is actually the opposite.[4] Jeremiah wrote, "But, though he cause grief," insinuating that God brings pain and suffering and fear. He went on to write, "He will have compassion according to the abundance of his steadfast love" (Lam. 3:32 ESV). In other words, suffering is something we can learn from when we believe God can and will respond. It sharpens our senses by burning away anything in our hearts and minds that is not for the purpose of glorifying God.

When we are honest about our suffering, pain, and fear, God's love helps us endure because it transforms us one step at a time. His love helps us understand that we don't need to be afraid of suffering—that it is a part of life and something that God can use to make us more transparent and approachable.

Recently, I lost a close relationship for complicated reasons. Through my pain and confusion, I prayed for God to heal the division, but that didn't happen. What I did realize was how I was placing too much emphasis on that friendship. The wisdom I gained from the loss of this relationship caused me to see my other friendships in a healthier light. Suffering shifts our attention to what's most important. As C. S. Lewis's famous saying reminds us, "God whispers to us in our pleasures, speaks in our conscience, but shouts in our pain; it is His megaphone to rouse a deaf world."[5]

After Huldah the prophetess shared with Josiah how God wanted the king's people to once again hear and obey his Word, Josiah used all of his power and energy to make right what was wrong. He rebuilt his kingdom by implementing the Word of God once again. Anything else he was working on went to the wayside. The Israelites were guilty of bowing down and worshiping pagan gods that had been introduced to them when they had first entered the Promised Land. But Josiah heard the Scriptures and purged the land of pagan priests and pagan gods. He did everything he could to obey God's Word; a wise move on his part.

When we are suffering, Scripture serves as a messenger of healing, sometimes correcting, exhorting, and encouraging, and many times reminding us of God's presence. When I'm in a season of suffering and I can't find my way, my spirit often utters, *Just one light, God*, and a Scripture verse then comes to mind and lights the step in front of me. "Ah," I say, "makes sense; sounds wise." I am then one step closer to the other side, with a few gold coins jingling in my pocket.

When We Don't Invite God into Our Own Suffering

Sadly, many incredible leaders and mature Christians are missing opportunities for honest and transparent conversations with the next generation because they don't know how to deal with their own suffering. They have never placed their broken selves in God's presence and asked him to search them or asked others to listen to him on their behalf.

It's not easy to experience pain or to have the first response of placing our broken selves in the presence of God. We must beg the Spirit of God to search our hearts during a time of suffering lest our pain cause us to hide our true selves. Unrefined pain hardens women's hearts. Pain that hasn't been sifted through the loving heart of God makes us lose our way, leaving us confused and disillusioned on the inside. Many times it is the reason behind the tendency to fix people when they share with us about a concern or problem.

The Tendency to Try to "Fix" Others

Until we learn how to respond to the suffering in our own lives, we will continue to try to fix people. When we experience God's searching of us and wait in his presence with a willingness to receive from Scripture personally, we can then respond to those who are suffering with more of God's heart and mind.[6]

This was the case for Diana, whose doctor told her, "You have an aggressive form of cancer." As the doctor explained the next steps and appointments, she knew this diagnosis would change her life—especially her relationship with God. By the time she hung up the phone, she had determined to invite God into every aspect of her disease. *God*, she prayed later that night, *I surrender my life into your capable hands.*

What caused more pain for her than the operation and chemo was the thought that her four-year-old daughter and infant son could be motherless. Diana leaned heavily on what God showed her through Scripture. These verses gave her hope and kept her from self-pity and bitterness. Years later, when I met Diana, she told me that what got her to the other side of her suffering was God's promises to her. "God didn't promise me a long life or even physical healing. But he did remind me that he's the Father to the fatherless. That's what I held on to when I was so sick day after day."

Diana did not focus on the statistics of cancer survivors. Instead she focused on truths that told her about God, particularly that he would never leave her or forsake her.[7] And she held him to those truths. What grounded her further were the scriptures of God's sovereignty in the midst of total chaos.[8] Believing he was in control settled her spirit. Because Diana trusted in what God gave her from Scripture while she was suffering through cancer, she can now offer wisdom without a need or desire to fix the hundreds of younger women who face similar battles.

False Knowledge and Understanding

When we follow the pattern laid out for us in Scripture while we are suffering, we will suffer well. Ironically, the two greatest barriers to suffering well are lack of knowledge and lack of understanding: we are fearful of not knowing enough to handle the problem and anxious when we don't understand what the future holds. Aren't those two things behind our desire to fix other people? So we overthink the suffering that has come to us instead of looking for what God has to say personally to us through Scripture.

It's our responsibility to make sure we are not offering others advice that contradicts Scripture or God's ways. What the younger generation needs is the "spiritual wisdom and understanding"[9] that come only from God, as true spiritual wisdom comes only through the Holy Spirit.

Living Out the Pattern of Sharing Wisdom

Authors Nicholas D. Kristof and Sheryl WuDunn are the creators of the brilliant book *Half the Sky: Turning Oppression into Opportunity for Women Worldwide.*[10] Focusing on three particular issues for the world's women—sex trafficking, gender-based violence, and maternal mortality—they offered solutions, such as girls' education and microfinance, for these tragedies. They have seen how outsiders can truly make a significant difference in the lives of women suffering these injustices. Their book gives example after example of women who have turned despair into hope. We as Christian women need to do the same by talking about how God has turned our own despair into hope.

Young women need us to connect their suffering with our own pain and faith stories. We need to tell them our own stories of infertility, abuse, rape, bankruptcy, job loss, unfaithful spouses, pornography addictions, drug addictions, poverty, gambling, eating disorders, poor body image, abortion, widowhood, grief, accidents, and disease. This gives us a chance to tell what God did for us and in us during our times of suffering; those listening will hear about Christian hope. This is how we model a biblical view of suffering.

When people hear despairing stories that are turned into hope, it encourages them to sink into the sovereignty of God. They can hear the wisdom others gleaned from a horrible time. All of us are bombarded with news of mass shootings, genocides, school bombings, female mutilation, and sex slavery. Such atrocities may have existed before, but now we know about them sooner and with more detail. The women behind us don't have the wisdom and experience we have gained from walking with God for more years. That is why it is so important that we share our stories. They matter.

Here are some specific things you can do to share the wisdom you have gained:

1. Tell your stories of suffering. I grew up in a church where people were given an opportunity to talk about what God was doing in their lives. On Sunday nights, the pastor would ask if anyone had a testimony. Inevitably there were tears and cliché comments about hope in Jesus. A few years later, when Brad and I were in deep grief, I remembered those stories as I developed a fresh vocabulary for tough times, and they reminded me that my pain had a purpose beyond me. The testimonies of my elders served as tiny headlamps, leading me out of utter darkness.

So talk with women about what Jesus has done in your life. Telling our stories of suffering and hope gives listeners a chance to ponder what God's role is in our suffering. It's that kind of introspection and reflection that the younger generation longs for.

Every time I share a story of my own suffering and what God gave me through it, women want to tell me their similar stories. It doesn't matter if I'm just having a private conversation or speaking publicly. Many women haven't told their stories of getting to the other side. I've found that my transparency breeds transparency in others. Telling our stories aloud takes away the fear of saying the truth and creates safe places for the women who are listening. They think, *I need to talk openly about what I've been through and stop keeping it hidden.*

2. Articulate Christ's work in your life every day. We need fresh ways to say how Jesus is our hope in overcoming the world's suffering. This happens best in everyday conversations. Just verbally being thankful for one thing in the day and recognizing that such a gift is from God are ways of passing along a godly attitude. We can also be honest with others about times when we did not forgive someone even though we knew this was what Christ taught.

Thinking godly about our answers to pain and suffering is a lost art. When we have conversations with other women, we must pass along biblical attitudes about suffering. As Kenda Creasy Dean wrote, "That reinforces the church's unique understanding of who God is in Jesus Christ."[11] It brings them healing.

3. Journal your stories. Writing forces us to organize and categorize our stories. It helps us articulate what happened and what we learned, sometimes bringing to our awareness things we hadn't even realized were in our stories.

Whenever I mentor writers at writing workshops, the majority of my conversations center on the person's journey or story. Each time, the writer shows up sheepishly, not thinking that she has anything to say. But that is never the case. Journaling can help you find your voice so you can tell your stories of suffering and pain to someone God brings along your path. As you tell a story, you will allow the listener to become introspective or thoughtful and you will get to hear once again how your suffering gave you wisdom.

Healing Bridges the Gap

It took Brad and me years before we could articulate God's goodness after Anthony and Elisa were killed. We gained wisdom about the way we lived our lives, the goals we set, and how we treated others who lost loved ones unexpectedly. Over and over again, the Spirit of God led us to humble ourselves, to ask others to pray, and to beg God to search our hearts. We leaned in to hear what God had to say about what was in our hearts. In the first year, I learned how God heals in time. I started to form a tenderness for Scripture instead of viewing it as a list of warnings. It's from this pattern of how to respond to suffering that I now draw close to the women in the next generation.

Last Christmas I received a phone call from a woman whose husband left her for another man. They had been married for twenty years and had raised four children, two still at home, and now she will finish raising the family on her own. When I pray with her, I focus on the facts and what step she must take next. When she insists on praying for her husband's restoration, I ask God to search her heart and I agree with her in prayer, as I know only God can change a person.

One of my relatives was diagnosed with a rare form of cancer soon after an excruciating battle with her bipolar husband who had died a year earlier. She is full of faith, the things of God, and hope. When we talk, we focus on what's good in life and in the world. "Why was my life so full of suffering?" she asks. As we enter into that question together, we both start seeing the good gifts God generously gave her, and I count them aloud for her. There's a wisdom in naming the good in the presence of suffering and pain. It's also an art.

Stories of other women come to mind as well. A dear friend who works as an oncology nurse at a large teaching hospital is facing a nasty divorce after discovering that her husband was cheating on her with various women for more than fifteen years. I walked alongside her in some dark moments as she realized her marriage had been a lie. Because of my own suffering, I knew it would take time for her to even want to heal. Often I was just present while she cried out to God for help. She just needed a witness to her pain.

Two friends have sons under eighteen who have life-threatening illnesses. One does not have a cure to this day. Her son is eight years old. Each of these women prays and seeks God, and I've been a part of the friend circle who prays for them. Their situations haven't been made perfect; in fact, I struggle with wanting to keep praying. As Philip Yancey wrote, "Somehow we must offer our prayers with a humility that conveys gratitude without triumphalism, and compassion without manipulation, always respecting the mystery surrounding prayer."[12] What I have witnessed is that the wisdom God gives from a time of suffering is always passed along to another—maybe not in an exact form, but something true and real is given. Such spiritual wisdom is worth more than gold.

But we can't offer this kind of wisdom if we haven't allowed God to heal us and change us, if we haven't submitted to the process we have been discussing in this chapter. If you have never surrendered your suffering to God and allowed him to search your heart and sift through what is there, it is not too late to do it now.

No matter how much time has passed since you first experienced suffering, you can still take the steps of getting to the other side.

Remember, none of us are immune to suffering; we cannot compare our suffering, but we must tell our stories. In this way we differentiate the pain and create vulnerability and we provide safe places for others to tell their own stories of pain. Think about the younger women in your life and what it is you want to pass along to them. Look at their lives, their concerns, their fears, and their hopes and dreams. Now look down the path you've walked with God all these years. The wisdom and spiritual insight you have dangling around your neck is the gold that has passed through the fire of suffering. Now it's time to give it away. And when you are in the presence of a younger woman who is desperate for your stories, as you begin the telling, as you begin to share your gold, her heart will whisper, *Thank you, God, for that one light.*

Chapter Four

The Power of Comfort

The Father of compassion and the God of all comfort, who
comforts us in all our troubles, so that we can comfort those in
any trouble with the comfort we ourselves receive from God.

Second Corinthians 1:3–4

I know what it means to desperately need reassurance, support, and comfort. My parents were first-generation Christians who had little or no role modeling of a healthy marriage. When they came to Christ, the church and parachurch organizations they were involved with were patriarchal in their approach to marriage, meaning the husband was the authority in the home and the wife was simply to submit to him.

My father was a devoted dad who took his new Christianity seriously, signing the family up for Christian camps, retreats, and church programs. He meant well, and each night we had a family time of Bible reading that lasted about an hour. But because there was no discussion, it was boring and hard to relate to; I spent my time daydreaming.

The earliest memories I can recall are of family gatherings with my dad's uncles, aunts, cousins, and their children, to whom I felt close. Dad's family struggled with poverty, and because he was determined not to do the same, he worked hard and saved his money.

My mother's upbringing was different. Her Jewish parents owned a tailor shop in downtown Philadelphia until her father was diagnosed with schizophrenia at thirty-three years old and placed in a mental institution. My mom was just a baby when this happened, but my grandmother signed Mom and her two young brothers over to the Jewish foster care system of Philadelphia. My grandmother's siblings and extended family were all business owners who lived nearby. Rumor had it that one sister offered to take the children, but my grandmother didn't want them to get "too attached to an aunt." Many years later, my grandmother decided she wanted her children back home with her, but the years of separation changed them all and it wasn't a happy reunion. Mom never really felt deeply loved or accepted by her family.

My parents met at Temple University. Two years after they married, they were introduced to Christ through a neighbor. As a Jewish woman (my mom went to Hebrew school when she was in foster care), Mom found it difficult to accept Jesus as Messiah. Yet she did. And it turned her into an evangelist.

The oldest of three children, I grew up feeling close to my mother. She sheltered me from my father's rigid ways. She talked openly with me about Jesus and often explained how miraculous it was for her to be saved. I experienced an enormous amount of security from my parents and our family in those days. My mom was involved at church, she prayed, and she was a good and compassionate woman in our community. But then she started getting sick a lot and staying home. She seemed less and less happy.

Because of health reasons and marital problems, my mom moved out of our house when I was fourteen years old. Years later, when we had a rare conversation about this, she admitted to having isolated herself. Mom could see that she had pulled away from the community of people who would have been able to comfort her.

Emotionally speaking, I was on my own once my mother left our home. Even in the middle of community, school, and church life, I felt abandoned and unprotected. I went from being surrounded by my mother's Jewish relatives and my father's Catholic family to having no one around. Once Mom wasn't there to make arrangements for us to get together with relatives, it seemed like no one knew how to relate to us. A handful of my aunts and cousins tried to connect with me during those years, but I wanted them to reach out to Mom.

One morning soon after my mother left, when I was a sophomore in high school, I sat among my peers in a US history class with tears falling from my eyes. The other students looked at me not knowing what to do or say. With my heart breaking, I willed myself to take copious notes. I resolved not to burden others with my sadness and learned how to project an image of independence to those around me. When a teenage girl plays sports, sings in choir, and leads a full social life, she can appear calm and collected to the adults around her. I was anything but. I needed to be comforted, but my teenage spirit believed something then that I only now can articulate: *I cannot rely on anyone else to be there for me at a deep level.*

Within five years of my family of origin falling apart, many of my extended family members died early from health problems.

Almost all of them were from Dad's side. Internally, my feelings were chaotic and I was in danger of starting life off with a flimsy, useless faith. The adults who taught me Jesus was the Way, the Truth, and the Life didn't seem to think he was enough. I wasn't very trusting of God and wondered what the point of Christianity was if it didn't help my family. Where was I supposed to learn how to live by faith?

When Comfort Is Absent

I needed comfort from women who weren't leaning on me to comfort them. I needed help so I could settle back down inside and remember who God made me to be, even though my world had been torn apart. I needed a reassuring friend who was willing to help me catch my breath. I didn't want others to feel sorry for me; I wanted someone to be present to my pain and to offer me consolation. Without comfort, my heart was in danger of drifting away from true Christianity. I really needed tender voices who could soothe my rebellious spirit, voices who would remind me that God didn't break up our family. (When you are young, comfort is as necessary as food—you need it every few hours.)

My heart was also in danger of getting hard. The intense emotions I felt when my family fell apart caused me to start forming harmful perspectives and habits. I vowed to be single so that I could protect myself from the deep hurt I'd experienced. I determined to work long hours and depend on God to meet my emotional needs. In other words, I assumed control over my life. I did not invite God into my pain, nor did I give him a chance to display his healing power in my life.

Self-reliance was my watchword. While in college I convinced all of my professors and my advisor that I could handle more than a full load of classes and also work selling advertising for the school newspaper. When my house of cards collapsed midsemester, everyone asked why I hadn't reached out for help. The answer? I hadn't wanted to burden anyone.

That is not to say I wasn't completely without comfort. Michelle and my girlfriends gave me comfort in my teen years. Later, Toni sheltered and protected my heart with her words. She had lost her own mother when she was in her early twenties. She didn't try to replace my mother, but she would often show up at just the right time. The way she talked about her own loss and recovery, the way she trusted God with her most private of feelings, gave me comfort. She'd lean over to me and say, "Pam, honey, you can't change what happened with your family. But you can choose to live your life differently." But those conversations happened after I graduated from college. It was difficult for me to articulate how I needed comfort when I was younger.

A Generation in Need of Healing Comfort

For years now, our nation has been hearing about the "lost" generation. The cynical faith crisis of Gen X ("They like Jesus but not the church"[1]), the shifting family values of up-and-coming leaders, the fact that Angelina Jolie is this generation's hero—all seem to reinforce that evangelical Christianity is running short on time in our culture. According to David Kinnaman, president of Barna Group, "The dropout problem is, at its core, a faith-development problem; to use religious language, it's a disciple-making problem. The church is not adequately preparing the next generation to follow Christ faithfully in a rapidly changing culture."[2]

Learning to receive and give comfort is one way we can "adequately prepare" the next generation of women who feel abandoned and unprotected by their families or the church. Comforting words ease pain and encourage women to hold on to their faith in a rapidly changing culture.

We must take off our everyday eyewear so we can see the new reality of where young women are. One study on the emerging adult culture reports that "by age 18 to 23, many emerging adults have endured their own or others' drug addictions, alcoholism, divorces, arrests, relational betrayals, frightening accidents, academic failures, job disappointments, parental abandonment, racism, and deaths of friends."[3] Many women still live with wounds and are recovering from the hard knocks of life.

They need someone to pay attention to why they are feeling what they are feeling and why they are acting the way they are acting. When they receive comfort, it enables them to make better choices. Comfort helps them hear the tender words God speaks to them in the midst of their discomfort. When a woman comforts another woman, she brings God's presence into that woman's feelings of hurt and fear.

One time I was present as a young woman who had just been released from prison prayed, "God, break my addiction to crack. Help me to stop wanting it." Another woman, a mature Christian, gently laid her hand on this woman's back and thanked God for the request, for his power to break the chain. Her soothing words filled the room, serving as sweet comfort to this woman whose ravished soul began to open up to her Creator's words.

But you and I cannot give comfort to other women unless we have been comforted ourselves, unless we have done the difficult and deep work of healing and sought Christ in the broken places so that we have some gold to share. In this era of looking like we have it all together, we need to remember to receive comfort for ourselves.

Receiving Comfort

In Isaiah 40:1–2, God said, "Comfort, comfort my people.… Speak tenderly to Jerusalem." What he speaks to us turns our "mourning into gladness." God promised, "I will give them comfort and joy instead of sorrow" (Jer. 31:13). But how do we receive God's comfort? We have to admit we are sitting in ashes with a spirit of despair. We must name what it is we need comfort for.

Few of us outgrow the need for comfort when we are hurting. Once a heart is broken, the longing for comfort doesn't change. The challenge is not letting our overwhelming feelings stay hidden. Unrefined feelings form a tight steel barrier around our hearts, and when that happens, we are not safe.

I am all too familiar with the vulnerable, tender need to be comforted by others outside my immediate family. In the fall of my junior year in college, three of my closest friends and I lived in a townhouse off campus. I became close friends with our roommate who was six years older than the rest of us. Her name was Sharon.

Often late into the evenings, Sharon and I would talk about our backgrounds, parents, siblings, and passions. Her ability in asking me specific questions about my family brought a comforting presence that to this day I know was from the heart of God. Soon after my dad had come to visit me in college, Sharon asked, "Pam, what do you think really happened with your parents? Do you think your dad and mom still love each other?" Most people are reticent to ask specific, pointed questions for fear they will upset the other person. Sharon's questions came alongside me, called me up, and called me out, helping to expose my pain and sadness. The power of healing comfort lies in an ability to ask a good question and to hang around long enough to help birth the answer.

In her book on the Holy Spirit, Catherine Marshall wrote about her experience of God as a tender, comforting mother to her when her husband, Peter, was having a heart attack. But later she recognized another dimension to God's comfort, "not only loving consolation, but strength."[4] I realize this is an example of God comforting a woman during a tragedy, but there's something for us to see. We don't just receive comfort through tender, soothing words alone. Women can receive comfort through strong, courageous words, empowering us to cope with the atrocities of life.

What comforted me the most as I learned to live with my mother's abandonment was when I believed who God said I was. At a Young Life camp, I heard I was a beloved daughter of the King. From my church youth group leaders, I heard that God was with me and created me with a purpose. In my early adult years, how I received comfort became more specific. During times of prayer in small groups or one-on-one, "words" were spoken to me. For instance, I've had to name aloud a broken heart, severe disappointments, and at times, sheer exhaustion. A comforting scripture, a prophetic word, or a reminder of who I was in Christ whispered aloud brought healing comfort. As adults, we can't expect others to read our minds, so we must name our grief out loud. This is not a sign of weakness, but of humility.

Another way we receive comfort is through our tears. Giving ourselves the freedom to cry in the presence of another soul opens us up to be comforted. Rather than apologizing and saying, "I'm really all right. I shouldn't cry like this," we can let our hearts swell with emotion and spill over so the contents can be shared. We learn what we need comfort for when we cry with another person. After years of running together, my girlfriend and I have few secrets between us. Yet I am still surprised when I get choked up while talking about my life with her. My tears indicate to both of us that something in me needs healing comfort; I don't hold my sadness back or swallow it back down.

Women who are comforted can comfort others. We are responsible to be meticulous when it comes to things of the faith, including our need to receive God's healing comfort. Yet in our misguided quest for spiritual independence, we have largely ignored this need. Consequently, the women coming up behind us don't know what to do with their sad feelings because our own hearts are hardened and unable to offer them comfort. As Kenda Creasy Dean wrote, "American young people are, theoretically, fine with religious faith—but it does not concern them very much, and it is not durable enough to survive long after they graduate from high school. One more thing: we're responsible."[5]

Living Out the Pattern of Healing Comfort

Jesus said, "Blessed are those who mourn, for they shall be comforted" (Matt. 5:4 ESV).

We must live out the pattern of comfort for the younger women in our lives, no matter the cause of their pain or discomfort. Jesus didn't classify the mourners whom we should comfort. It doesn't matter who is at fault for the pain. We can comfort younger women even when they are acting in ways we don't approve of or understand.

In Scripture, the Greek word for "comfort" is *parakaleo*, meaning "to the side of," with *kaleo* meaning "to call." The word's intent is to help, comfort, encourage—it's a kind of call with a particular effect. When a young woman tells you what her pain is, comfort her. It's what she needs and nothing more.

If we are going to build trust with the next generation, then our approach to offering healing comfort must follow the pattern of God's own heart toward his people. He didn't desert them when they were in need of comfort; his desire to give to them was stronger than the reasons why they got to such a bad place.

Hosea 2:14–15 describes how God restored Israel when she was furthest from him. Although Israel turned her back on the One who loved her most, worshiped other gods, and suffered all alone in her captivity, God pursued her and cared about how she was feeling. He saw how troubled she was because of her deep wound, and he desired to do good to her.

> Therefore I am now going to allure her; I will lead
> her into the wilderness and speak tenderly to her.

There I will give her back her vineyards, and will
make the Valley of Achor a door of hope.

When God offers healing comfort, he touches the soul with all of its messiness and hardness and confusion. Love comforts, which was why the psalmist cried in Psalm 119:76, "May your unfailing love be my comfort."

Ways of Expressing Healing Comfort

Offering healing comfort isn't the same as feeling bad for someone. It's not comforting to show pity or to say you will pray and then walk away from the person and her pain. It's not comforting if you listen to someone tell you about her pain and then launch into a story about yourself or someone else with a similar wound.

What brings comfort? Words of care and concern. Instruction about how to move forward. Physical touch helps. Food helps. When healing comfort is at its best, it's a work of the Holy Spirit. It's the work of someone who feels an urgent need to connect with the hurting person.

Here are some things you can do to comfort.

Persuade, Don't Preach

Soon after I wrote an article for *Christianity Today*'s Her.meneutics website[6] asking younger women to forgive the older generation for not relating well to their needs, someone in my community wrote me an email that only reinforced my message. In the article, I quoted the younger women admitting how our interactions with

them are not comforting. I said we were sorry and asked if they
would please forgive us. After reading my article, this older woman
said she thought the girls I was writing about needed counseling!
Rather than thinking deeply about her own actions and how to
offer healing comfort to the younger women in her life, this woman
wanted to preach a different message: get some help. Ironically, her
judgmental response was exactly the kind of reaction young girls
"sense" or "feel" from older women. We need to learn the art of
persuasion so we can first get close enough in hopes that young
women will open their hearts to us. Preaching or telling people to
get help pushes them away.

Persuading a woman, or as Hosea speaking for God said, "I
am now going to allure her," means that we speak tenderly to her
soul. Last year, my friend called to say her teenage daughter was
expelled from school because she was caught using drugs and now
was up in her room not responding to anyone. She wondered if I
could talk with her daughter. Before I drove to their home, I sent
the young girl a text, "Want to chat?" She texted back, "My parents
are idiots." I then texted, "How about I come over?" "Sure" was all
I got. So I sat with her in her room for about thirty minutes saying
good things to her heart. As a mother would comfort a crying baby,
I used a quiet, soothing voice as I gently and carefully spoke to her.
I'm not convinced it was so much what I said but how I spoke to a
heart that was getting hard. I allured her to a place where her heart
could be soft again. Persuading someone to open her heart is the
only way lasting, healing comfort can start. Before I left, I made
eye contact with her and said, "I give you permission to text or call

me anytime day or night if you need to." She did text me one time, and all she needed was reassurance that I meant what I had said.

The only way a wounded human heart opens is through kindness, not through preaching or shock and judgment. We persuade with kindness. When you see the disparity between a woman's complaints and what she's doing to ease them, do not preach to her about what she needs to change. Instead, persuade her with your loving presence. Do you hear a younger woman complain about someone using "just take it to the old rugged cross" language with her? Don't let offense come; instead, let her hear the sound of a voice from one who has been comforted by God. Persuade her to tell you what's going on and let your presence send the same message.

Set Aside Time for One-on-One

After God allured Israel into the desert so he could be alone with her, he spoke tenderly to her. God's love compelled him to be with his people without distraction. He didn't use their bad choices, their awful circumstances, or their sin as an excuse to leave them alone. Instead, he saw their discomfort as an opportunity to get them alone—so he could give them the attention he longed to give them.

Looking back to my early adult years, I can see how God used one-on-one times with women ahead in life to bring me healing comfort. Often I found comfort when someone invited me for a meal or when we met together in a restaurant. When a hurting person sets aside time to be alone for conversation, that's when she recognizes some of her most basic needs.

Women who have deep wounds from the tragedies we listed earlier often feel like Elijah did when he went into the desert praying he might die: "I have had enough, LORD.... Take my life" (1 Kings 19:4). Having Elijah all by himself, God comforted him by baking him bread and offering him a jar of water.

Listen with Wonder

It was after his physical needs were met that Elijah and God had an incredible one-on-one conversation where God listened to Elijah with wonder. When a young woman needs comfort, let her transparency ignite a sense of wonder in you—a sense of astonishment at the lively inner feelings that may match your own. The more she can express her feelings, violent and bitter as they may be, the greater the opportunity will be for you to ask her specific questions and to reveal God's comfort in your own sufferings. It's right there, in that face-to-face safe haven, that the gospel of Christ can be received and a young woman's faith can be supported and strengthened rather than remain flimsy and useless. In the most tender of voices say, "I'm so, so sorry this happened to you." Comfort her by being alone with her, offering her food and drink, and listening to her with wonder.

Pray with Pure Motives

I am deeply moved when I read the apostle Paul's parting words to the Thessalonians: "Because we loved you so much ... we worked night and day in order not to be a burden.... We dealt with each of you as a father deals with his own children, encouraging, comforting and urging you to live lives worthy of God" (1 Thess. 2:8–12). Welling up deep inside me is the awareness that our motives for caring for the women in our lives aren't always as pure as Paul's were. Something lurking in us causes us to comfort others for our own purposes. Paul once killed flesh and blood from pure hate. Later, he pursued flesh and blood from pure love; I want motives like that. The next generations of women need us to have motives like that when we pray for God's comfort.

When I first heard Staci was angry with me, I was livid. How could she pull away from me when I was constantly reaching out, leaving messages, letting her know I cared about her? As soon as I could, I drove to her house early one Saturday morning and confronted her in her kitchen. "What have I done that could make you upset at me like this?" I said.

Stirring the oatmeal while tears streamed down her cheeks, she told me, "I don't feel comforted when you tell me you're praying for me. How do you know what to pray for me unless you are face-to-face with me?"

Her words stung me.

Five months earlier Staci had lost her son, Alex, in a tragic car accident, and the second I received the call, I was in her living room, holding her and her family. For several days, Staci's extended family and friends became my own as I helped with funeral arrangements. Staci had been on my heart and mind, and I had made sure to let her know it.

But as I reflected on what she had said, I realized that she was right in feeling hurt by me. Had I been calling and texting her in order to support and comfort her? Or so I could tell myself that I was doing what I could to help her? Was I calling and texting just to make myself feel better? I realized that to indeed comfort Staci, I had to pray with her and for her differently. My motives needed to change. Was I willing to let what happened to her change my life? If so, I had to comfort her in ways that actually did that!

Any woman who has suffered loss will tell you how often people comfort them for themselves. True healing comfort, the kind God gave to the Israelites when he allured them into the desert and spoke tenderly to them, is a comfort that gives something. It's a comfort that restores the hole left by the burning fire of drug addiction, abortion, divorce, abandonment, death, and failure and sin.

Inspire Hope

What God gave his wandering lover was hope, hope that she would once again lift her voice and sing. When we comfort another, our words and prayers give hope that she will get through the pain and desperation she is feeling.

Sometimes I sing my prayers for women. When Jill realized her house was in foreclosure, she could barely speak. She asked if I would pray for her. I sat at the piano and sang out to God to comfort the woman who knelt beside the piano, waiting for a healing touch from the Spirit. At times, it's God's presence that gives hope and comfort more than our words.

Something to Remember

As we reach out and offer comfort to this next generation, we must recognize that they might not see themselves as spiritual as we see ourselves. But many do consider themselves leaders[7] and are more likely than us to take on leadership roles. We need to be prepared for their high sense of self. Women who are brimming with strength and confidence still need comfort.

Living out the pattern of healing comfort means we will not hold back when we discover that the young woman is the vice president of a bank at twenty-eight years old or that she's had multiple sexual partners or just served time in prison for identity theft. The honest and humbling truth is that these young women are more likely to teach us more about Jesus Christ and his will for this world than we have learned from the way we've been doing church in America.

While I was writing this chapter, our small community experienced the shock of a thirty-eight-year-old married woman of two going missing and then taking her own life with no warning signs. Although I didn't know her personally, I sat in the back of the small brick church for a gathering to honor her life. The pastor read aloud a letter from the woman's mother. In her letter, the stunned and grieving mother said that not in a million years could she imagine her daughter making a decision like she did. Urgent in her tone, the mom concluded with a persuasive call: if you are a mother, aunt, sister, girlfriend, or daughter, please take the time to be a friend and comfort someone, even if you don't think she looks like she needs an encouraging word, a spirit lifted, or a few minutes of conversation, because you just don't know the intense feelings of sadness or brokenness someone may have. I left the building wondering how we could increase our expressions of comfort to one another in a world where so many value their "privacy." I pray that not one woman in your life and mine would ever think that we would deem her weak when we see her struggling. May our lives tell her, "You have a friend in me and are deeply loved."

Chapter Five

Acting with Understanding

At a certain point, I just felt, you know, God is not looking for alms,
God is looking for action.

Bono

When my friend Terri heard about a young woman in her community who was pregnant and considering an abortion, Terri knew she needed to act. She had had three abortions before she got married and wanted to tell this young woman her experience. Terri and Ashley met in Terri's home.

Terri said, "You cannot believe the guilt I live with all these years later. I know the depression I suffer is from the decision to end those lives. The man I was dating paid for the abortions, and I don't know if I can ever forgive him."

Ashley listened intently, then said, "But I'm not very far along."

Terri later shared with me that although she knew that having an abortion wasn't God's way, in her conversation with Ashley she focused on her inability to forgive herself. She shared how she was tormented night and day by guilt over what she had done. Later, when she found out that Ashley had decided to have her baby, Terri told her, "That was the right sacrifice to make."

Terri acted with understanding, and because she did, Ashley made a life-giving choice. Tragically, many women facing similar choices don't get the kind of intervention that Ashley received from Terri.

This was the case for a woman in her late thirties who asked me to pray with her at a women's conference. She told me that she was struggling with anger and resentment for having aborted two of her pregnancies. The first time she had an abortion she was unmarried and way too young to rear a child. Her boyfriend agreed with her. The second time, she was married but felt the timing to have a baby was wrong. As she talked with me about those isolating times, she sounded disillusioned and defeated.

I was saddened by this woman's story because it told me that the women in her life had missed something. They had not been there for her when she stood at a crossroads; they had failed to act with understanding toward her. If they had, they could have been there to help her make good choices regarding her pregnancies.

Titus 2:3–4 speaks about women ahead in the race: "Teach what is good, and so train the young women" (ESV). The Greek word used for "train" in this verse is *sophronizo*, which means "to call one to her senses, to make sensible." The world has become a noisy and competitive place. Making the most of one connection with another person is a way of seeking to understand that person. We have no idea what God is up to in that person's life, but we can be a part of it if we take the time. As Terri's conversation with Ashley shows, God can use one conversation, one interaction, to change a person's course.

Why It's Important

As we work toward becoming safe havens, we must change our mind-set and stop assuming that the women we know don't have needs or that they don't need friendship and understanding. The superwoman myth is over. The false and damaging persona of spiritual independence is a lie. Past writers and current researchers have noted that our spiritual health is dependent on intergenerational relationships.[1] When we relate to someone who is older, we see our lives through a long historical perspective of life as opposed to relying solely on our own experiences.

Well-known women such as Harriet Beecher Stowe and her sister Catharine Beecher held Americans to high moral standards because they wanted them to be responsible and assume the character of Christ. These great, thinking Christian women wrote of the obligations men and women have to themselves, their families, and their fellow citizens. One such obligation they described as denying self in order to be kind and good. The Beecher sisters were saying not only is it better for us to be concerned about the welfare of others, even those outside our families, but it's also a character quality of Christ.[2]

Could it be that our spiritual independence is keeping us from understanding what the women in our lives need and then acting on their behalf? I think many of us have bought into the spiritual independence that our Christian culture encourages. God's ways, however, are different. He can give us the right thoughts and plans for those who desperately need our attention—or even our intervention.

What We Should Do

When it comes to our relationships, we need to gain understanding for two reasons: to discern or to perceive what's going on with another person, and to do what's right for that person.

While it's true that no one except Christ can understand our circumstances and know us inwardly, it's also true that women need other women to understand them, to get them, to know them, and when necessary, to act on their behalf. It's our job to do everything in our power to let another woman know we understand her—that we see what she is up against and what her world is like.

Understanding is a gift God gives in divine moments. It's a burst of insight and discernment designed specifically for that situation. Unlike the wisdom we gain from suffering that helps us persevere in the long haul, understanding prompts us to a particular action.

The woman I talked with at the conference needed a few discerning women in her life who could say to her, "Stop! There's another way to live your life. You don't have to get an abortion. Instead, you can see yourself in a different light; you can make a better choice as you see the narrow path God has for you at this crossroads." The point is we need to be the person at the right place and at the right time.

A Biblical Model: Abigail

Before becoming king, but after his anointing, David spent a lot of years running from Saul. In 1 Samuel 25, David found meaningful work to do while he and his men were running in the wilderness; they formed a kind of watch group. Besides defending from lions and bears, this group protected themselves and others from robbers, criminals, and muggers. It was in this context that David encountered Nabal, a wealthy landowner whose name ironically means "fool."

One day, ten of David's men approached Nabal and asked for food. Why not? They had generously protected Nabal's land and his herdsmen from thieves for a time. Fool that he was, Nabal's response to David's polite request was beyond a no. Nabal was so rude he belittled David's family line. When he heard about it, David vowed and threatened disaster on Nabal's entire estate. David was ready to kill, to take revenge with his own hands.

But someone was there at the right place and at the right time: Abigail. She was convinced that the health of the Jewish nation and her family depended on her to act. She had a deep feeling of obligation, not just to a few people, but to everyone in her sphere of influence. Whether her intervention with David was solely for David's best interest is not the point. How she showed up and what she said at this crossroads in David's life model how an intelligent woman uses understanding at an opportune time.

As Proverbs 13:15 says, "Good judgment wins favor." Abigail used discernment in a crisis, and while her wise and successful ways may seem cunning, they were not. Abigail was able to make the most of her one connection with David and stop him from making a horrible mistake. I love how Eugene Peterson recreated the Abigail and David story:

> Abigail on her knees in the wilderness, on her knees
> before David. David is rampaging, murder in his
> eyes, and Abigail blocks his path, kneeling before

him. David has been insulted and is out to avenge
the insult with four hundred men worked up into a
frenzy. Abigail, solitary and beautiful, kneels in the
path, stopping David in his tracks.[3]

Here's what Abigail did and what we can do.

Living Out the Pattern of Understanding

Be Present to What Is Happening around You

Abigail was a prominent woman who managed her household and
business details with good management skills. She paid attention to
what was going on in the lives and conversations of those she came
in contact with. Her servant, upon hearing of David's threat and
the impending doom, said to her, "I need you to understand this,
to really get this; don't miscalculate. Dig deep so you can recognize
what's about to happen."

Because she was present to her servant, Abigail discovered what
had happened between David and her fool of a husband. Because she
lived in the everyday with her servants, Abigail was approachable.
Clearly, her servant knew her daily routine and the ways in which she
operated when he said, "Now think it over and see what you can do"
(1 Sam. 25:17). Abigail spent her days talking about ordinary things
with ordinary people. She reflected on the everyday matters of life
with her family and her servants, and she acted on what she learned
by making a plan.

Abigail stands in stark contrast to the way many people respond
in a dire situation. We might be tempted to spend our days thinking

of how things should have been, which creates discontentment, or we might obsess about how things will unfold, which is called worry. Both worry and discontentment destroy our abilities to reflect and live in the everyday.

I've found that heaven and earth intersect for me most often when I'm solving an outrageously practical problem in my ordinary life. When I "think it over and see what" I can do, I get understanding: I see the need for action.

Erwin McManus in his book *Chasing Daylight* talked about divine moments: "When you seize divine moments, you instigate an atomic reaction. You become a human catalyst creating a divine impact."[4] Abigail seized a divine moment.

What Abigail did and said next shows us the pattern of living out understanding in a serious situation where our spirits say, "God, your ways and thoughts are so different from mine. Give me your understanding, teach me, and give me a plan." And God did; he gave her a plan.

Enlist Help, If Needed

Abigail's plan included feeding David and his men, who had been on the run from Saul and were hungry and tired. Scripture says she "acted quickly" (1 Sam. 25:18). She did not hesitate. She took enough bread, wine, sheep, and raisin cakes to feed David and his men and loaded the goods on donkeys.

While I don't think Abigail was trying to tear down the superwoman myth (after all, the concept and word didn't even exist!), she didn't try to implement her plan all by herself. She recognized the job was too big for her alone, and she enlisted the help of her servants to get it done.

We can do something similar by asking God to open our eyes for the younger women who are five, ten, or twenty years younger than we are and want to support us. Sheri does a good job of inviting younger and older women to join her when she holds women's conferences in the Pacific Northwest. Her most recent committee has two women in their twenties, two in their thirties, one in her forties, and one in her seventies. Sheri is tearing down the false image that she can do things all on her own.

God often calls us to something that is bigger than we are, and we need to take note when divine understanding says, "You cannot do this on your own." God works wonders in impossible situations. I was reminded of this truth one Saturday evening when a neighbor came over and knocked on the front door. When I opened it, she stepped inside and began to sob. In between her crying and talking, I learned that her husband had had to leave town to take a new job and that she was left to load up the moving truck on her own. She had no one to help her. After I consoled her, I sent her home and said I would see what I could do. In a burst of insight and discernment, I realized I couldn't help her by myself and immediately enlisted the help of neighbors I knew. I sent out emails, texts, and calls, explaining this neighbor's plight. None of us knew her well, but the next day close to twenty neighbors showed up to what looked like an impossible situation. Within two hours, the group had helped load most of her belongings onto her moving truck.

Be Yourself, Not an Image

While Abigail sent her servants ahead with the food, she didn't send a servant in her place to approach David. She didn't send a messenger saying, "David, don't do this; you're going to regret it!" She brought her authentic self to talk directly to David. When she saw him, she hurried off her donkey, fell at his feet, and said, "On me alone, my lord, be the guilt" (1 Sam. 25:24 ESV). She then explained why David shouldn't kill her. "Look," she said, "I'm humble. I've brought you food, and I'm a woman traveling alone."

To be honest, I wouldn't naturally respond to the threat to murder my family and household the way Abigail did. I would have jumped off my donkey, huffed and puffed as I marched to face David, and said, "Back off!" In the case of David and Nabal, that wasn't God's way. Abigail's wise response showed that she was listening to God and that he gave her understanding.

When we are engaging with women who are younger than we are, we can think we need to have all the right answers and even use a certain language. In our efforts to be spiritual, we say to a woman in crisis, "Just take it to the cross; surrender it all. I'm praying for you." Or to show we understand, we talk about the facts of that crisis. But the understanding Abigail showed to David was the kind that spoke directly to his heart: "Please let your servant speak ... hear [me].... Please ..." (1 Sam. 25:24, 28 ESV). Abigail was vulnerable with David and let him see how she really felt—that he was in danger of losing his crown (vv. 23–29).

Similarly, when we are talking to a woman in crisis, we must express how much we care about her, without concern that it might come out wrong or make us feel awkward. We have to put aside our ideas about the way we want others to see us. We must resist these inclinations and be honest and authentic, even if it means sharing our mistakes and stumbles. When we have understanding, we realize those times when the most helpful thing we can say to a younger woman is that we don't have things all together.

My friend Jillian, days before speaking at her first retreat, called with this request: "Pam, think back to your first retreat. What practical advice would you give me?" Thinking back sixteen years to that conference required me to dig deep! I told her a couple of things that only experience could bring. I shared with her how years ago, I felt the need to protect myself at retreats. Often I wouldn't get to know the women, sometimes relying on the other team members to interact with the group. I missed out because I wasn't open. My behavior changed late one night when a shy woman came knocking at my door. It took her five minutes to tell me what was on her mind. Finally, she said, "I think you're holding back from us all the Spirit wants to give us when you stay in your room."

My vulnerability encouraged Jillian. She appreciated that I was real with her and said, "That helps me to pay more attention to what really matters—the women."

Think about Your Words

When Abigail asked for David's forgiveness on behalf of her rude husband, she did so with goodness-filled language. Reasoning again from God's point of view, Abigail said, "The LORD has kept you from bloodshed" (1 Sam. 25:26). Abigail understood that the pathway to David's heart was through his history. She knew Saul's history with David, and she knew David was preparing to be the future king. Spoken words can shape us and fill us, altering our perspective, and that was the case with David. He began worshiping

God: "Praise be to the LORD, the God of Israel, who has sent you today to meet me" (v. 32). This change came about as Abigail spoke about God's goodness to him.

Abigail took the blame (again) for her foolish husband and at the same time saw David's rage in light of his promised future: "The LORD your God will certainly make a lasting dynasty for my lord" (v. 28). In other words, don't ruin your future! Abigail referred to a specific promise God had made to David.

An excellent question to ask a younger woman who's standing at a crossroads is "What was God's last promise to you? Tell me about it. Tell me the circumstances surrounding that promise." Use goodness-filled language to rephrase that promise in her current crisis.

A woman did this for me several years ago, and her words were life-giving. Brad had been rushed to the hospital because he was extremely sick. After hours of doctors in and out of his room performing various tests, I started to panic and walked out the door to sit in the waiting room. Sitting there praying for us was a woman from my Bible study who was a few years older than I was. Seeing that I wasn't handling things well, she said, "Pam, tell me what you're thinking." As my panic-stricken words filled the air, she did something I will always remember. She stood close to me and said, "Do you remember last week when you told all of us how God keeps showing you he's watching over Brad?" I did remember; she helped me re-remember. Somehow her goodness-filled language pushed panic out of the way of controlling my heart; it was still there but much quieter as I whispered, "Thank you, God, that you are watching over Brad."

Don't Hold Back

Abigail found the narrow way David needed to take and steered him away from the wide and easy way that led to destruction. By not holding back from intervening in David's life, Abigail used discernment in keeping David from taking revenge. He was angry and could easily have told his men to slaughter Abigail and her servants right there on the spot. Yet, she got him to accept "from her hand what she had brought him" (1 Sam. 25:35). He heard her words and granted her request.

Most important, she changed David's view of himself. When Abigail arrived on the scene, David was warrior, seeing himself only as fighter, skilled in killing. What Abigail did by not holding back all she was and all she had was cast David in his eternal light; she helped him see the David God was preparing as king. She became a ray of light to the narrow path for David.

After David worshiped God for sending Abigail his way, he thanked her for her good judgment (1 Sam. 25:33). We need to do for other women what Abigail did for David. When we know a woman is standing at a crossroads, about to make a bad decision, we cannot hold back any good we have. We can't be vague or make subtle suggestions. We must shine light on the narrow path, pointing and saying, in effect, "Do you really want to live with blood on your hands the rest of your life? Let God take revenge and you go here."

Just as God used Abigail to change how David saw himself, he can use us to help another woman view herself in a life-giving way. A teacher I know saw scars on a student's arms and knew the student was cutting herself. When the teacher approached the student and asked her why she was in so much emotional pain, she heard, "I miss my old school with all my friends and the cutting helps me to not feel the pain." Not wasting one minute or holding back any love, the teacher took the student aside and, using goodness-filled words, said, "You can always tell me how you feel, but I want to introduce you to some new friends I think are a lot like you." Within a short amount of time, this teacher helped the young girl see herself differently, as someone who could start over. With a divine understanding, the teacher connected students to this new girl and helped her see herself in a different light.

Are you fearful of standing out as Abigail did? It takes grit and determination to stand with others as they decide to walk the narrow road. It feels like a contradiction to say that living out the pattern of understanding may put us in a dangerous situation. Abigail wasn't afraid to act on the divine understanding that she had received about David, even though it meant risking her life. She understood the situation was perilous, not only for her family, but for David and the kingdom of Israel as well. Had David taken revenge that day, it could have cost him his crown. Even worse, he could have been killed, leaving Israel without God's chosen king.

Partnering with God

Younger women need to have understanding women in their lives. When, like Abigail, we live in real time and demonstrate understanding, we will have opportunities to be in relationship with younger women. As God gives us insight about how to respond to a specific need, we need to focus on that and let the rest go. He is in the business of protection and promotion. We don't need to spend our lives preoccupied with how we will be safe or how we will be perceived.

When we hear someone is about to make or is making poor decisions, we must act quickly in going to that person. The key is to check our own ways and understanding at the door and to wait for God's perspective on the situation. He gives it while we are acting; he reveals the path while we are taking the next step. He provides the energy while we are exercising every ounce of energy and power we have to reach out to the women closest to us. When we live out the pattern of understanding, like the psalmist, we will see how we commend God's works to another generation. It's another way of passing along our faith, because we've partnered with God in keeping another person's path straight.

Chapter Six

Knowing Full Forgiveness

If You, Eternal One, recorded each offense, Lord, who
on earth could stand innocent? But with You forgiveness
exists; that's why true respect of You might flow.

Psalm 130:3–4 (VOICE)

When bad things happen to us, we sometimes make bad decisions and then try to justify those decisions. We think, *Well, if that hadn't happened to me, I wouldn't have needed to ease the pain with alcohol, or work, or overexercising*—or whatever "drug" it is we choose.

When my family fell apart, my drug of choice was a need to control the circumstances and even people in my life. At first this wasn't a conscious choice; it was just something I did in order to minimize the likelihood that I would be disappointed or hurt in some way. Even so, my need to control was damaging to my relationships. This became crystal clear to me when my oldest daughter turned fourteen (the age I was when my mother left) and my need to control her kicked into high gear.

I would look at Michaela and find myself unable to treat her like a fourteen-year-old should be treated. I became obsessed with making sure she felt secure. Once after Michaela spent the evening with a group of friends from her high school, I asked her how it went. As she listed off the different places and people involved, I became tyrannical in asking questions. "Whose car were you in? Were you with the guys? Did the girls stick together? Is that what you wanted to do?" At one point, she looked at me and said, "Mom, you're thinking too much about how I feel." Maybe those are normal questions for a parent to ask a teenager, but where I was heading with those questions wasn't good for either of us.

I realized I needed help in trusting my daughter and the person she'd become outside of what happened to me at her age. I sought professional help and placed myself in front of a counselor. After a few sessions, the counselor helped me see that my high need to control was a reaction to the chaos of my teen years and a way of protecting myself from pain. However, I was hurting my daughter rather than helping her, and my need to control was a sin. I needed to face where I was wrong and ask my daughter's forgiveness.

I also started to accept that I too was broken and in need of forgiveness. Outside of what happened with my mom, I'm a broken human being because of the fall. And that makes me a sinner, not a victim of someone else's sin. Unless I started facing why I had bad behaviors and became willing to forgive myself, how could I be a safe haven for my daughter?

Forgiveness Unblocks Our Hearts

The weeks and months after my mother left our home, I lived with a lot of shame because I no longer felt protected by her. And I didn't know how to care for my father and two younger siblings. The first time I went to visit her in her new home was a disaster. In my fourteen-year-old mind, I had decided to make the best of an awful situation and to act as if everything was fine when I got there. Mom had rented a room from an old family friend—the kind you think is a distant relative but you really don't know. I grabbed a ride to where Mom was living two towns away, walked up the steps to the house, and knocked on the door. As she led me to her bedroom, not talking about anything important, I had an overwhelming desire to beg her to come home. But when I sat on her bed and looked at her, I knew she didn't want to hear what I was feeling. She had other things on her mind.

Within an hour, I could hardly breathe and told Mom I had to leave. She never asked why and didn't try to stop me. A girl from my school lived two streets away, so I walked to her house hungry and, worse, feeling unwanted. My friend and her family served as a distraction to my pain for a few brief hours as we ate dinner, finished homework, and played games. Because it snowed that evening, my friend's mom insisted I spend the night. The next morning, wearing borrowed clothes two sizes too big, I walked toward my school locker and hung my head. Just as the oversized clothes made me feel unkempt, the shame I felt from being abandoned by my mom caused me to feel uncomfortable, distracted, and unlovely—no matter what I did to try to fit in.

From that point forward, stripping off every layer of that shame became my focus and my goal. I decided to stop expecting my mom to take care of me so that I would avoid the pain when she didn't. That cloak of self-preservation worked for a while; I distanced myself from her emotionally and accepted that this was how I would live.

A few years later, as a college student, I became aware of a dark place in my heart—a place that prevented me from getting close to others and from growing spiritually. Even though I had gained enough emotional distance from my mom that I could function normally, I lived with a continual sense of angst. Mom kept in touch with me through phone calls, occasional cards, and packages, but I made sure I didn't need her or make her feel obligated to me. That's when I realized that I had a problem and that if I didn't learn to forgive her for abandoning our family, I would continue to harden my heart toward others. The longer I lived without forgiving my mom, the longer the angst would eat away at me, holding me back from the good life God had for me.

When we don't forgive, something dark arrests our hearts. We continue to hurt people, no matter how the relationship is defined, because whatever is dark and blocking our hearts has a life of its own.

I know a woman who is thought of as a tremendous Christian. Through years of service and hard work, she has contributed to amazing causes and people in need; it's hard to find a woman more dedicated to the church. However, the unspoken truth among the women closest to her is that she is difficult to be around. Everything will be seemingly fine and running smoothly, when suddenly she goes silent, leaves the room, or just shuts down. This behavior makes people feel uncomfortable and uncertain when they are around her.

It was her daughter-in-law who confessed to me, "It's clear she hasn't forgiven someone along the way; I don't know if it's a parent, or maybe it's just herself."

Unfortunately, the real world doesn't teach us about the skill of forgiveness. Many people understand forgiveness as a onetime decision. It's not. We need the Spirit of God to help us forgive from our hearts. As Christians, we know it's the right thing to forgive, but without the Spirit's help, we rely on our natural inclinations. The more we rely on the Spirit to show us who we need to forgive and why, the less prickly and unsafe we will be toward others, because forgiveness softens our hearts and fills us with compassion. Learning to forgive isn't just about us feeling better; it's also about showing the world that God is alive and working, because forgiveness is only possible through him.

I believe we need the help of the Holy Spirit in order to obey God's command to forgive. We can't just will ourselves free from resentments and bad behaviors. We need the Spirit of Christ to empower us to experience forgiveness as a choice, as a continual attitude, and as a way toward truth. That was certainly the case for me.

The Spirit Helps Us Choose Forgiveness

In my college dorms, one room was reserved as the prayer room. Every morning at 6:00 a.m., I prayed through the Psalms as the words matched my own inner turmoil and need for God's help. On the morning I prayed Psalm 130, I cried out from a deep, dark place, pleading with God to help me forgive my mom. I told him I still loved her and sensed God was speaking to me about staying close to her. What wasn't clear to me then but is now is that God was encouraging me to choose to stay committed to the relationship. I wasn't certain I wanted that—it was too painful to want something from someone who wasn't capable of giving it. He wasn't telling me I *had* to stay in the relationship; the sense was that if I did and if I learned to wait on him, he would continue to give me a heart of forgiveness. I chose to forgive my mom that day, and forgiveness opened the door for me to move to another place with her and for me to grow spiritually.

But here's the truth: Because our relationship was broken and my mom didn't change, she was still able to hurt me. And when she did, my heart would once again come to a halt unless I forgave her. As I did, God, through the power of the Holy Spirit, filled in the gaps with other relationships that were healthy, with people who didn't hurt me in the same way.

Forgiveness Is Ongoing

Just as the beating of our hearts and the pressure of our blood are foundational to our overall heath, so is ongoing forgiveness foundational to our spiritual health. God helped me to keep choosing forgiveness, from that season of my life through the seasons of getting married, having children, working, rearing children, relocating around the country, and facing middle age.

Even though I had forgiven my mom that first time, old wounds would sometimes surface in unexpected places. For instance, I was talking with a young woman who wanted counsel on how to handle her mom's intervening presence while she was raising four young children. The more I listened to her, the more I wanted to stand up and shout, "Do you have any idea the gift you have? You are upset because your mom wants to *help* you?" Once alone, I was riddled with self-pity and I couldn't shake it. I went to my room, shut the door, and knelt by my bed. *Holy Spirit, I need more of your power to help me let go of resentment about what I never had from my own family when my girls were small. I need help in forgiving the whole situation.* God helped me make that choice in that moment, not just for my own healing, but also for the other women in my life who would know God better the healthier I became.

Just as Jacob wrestled God all night asking for a blessing, so must we wrestle with forgiveness so that we can relate to others out of hearts of love and openness rather than out of a need to hide or to defend and protect ourselves. But an ongoing wrestling it is. We must wrestle with God through the night hours, not letting the sins of shame and bitterness overtake us. We must hold on until God responds and enables us to forgive, removing the blockage and pumping fresh blood and life into our spiritual veins.

When I was first married and something happened between my mom and me that covered me in the familiar shame, I was tempted to cut her off because I didn't want the relationship I had with her to poison my marriage. As I wrestled with God in prayer about what to do, I pictured my mom as an orphan living in a foster home as a child. Overcome with compassion for her, I felt God was saying she would need me and that she had done the best she knew how. Understanding this and forgiving her enabled me to stay in the relationship—albeit with some protective boundaries in place—and kept my heart open to others.

Forgiveness Frames Our World in Reality

Forgiveness purifies us and makes us blameless, but it doesn't always change the situation. That's reality. But sometimes our Christian culture communicates a different message, one that says all we need to do is forgive and everything will work out perfectly.

This was brought home to me a few years ago when a former student from Pennsylvania called me and said her marriage was in trouble. Through her tears and sobs, she said her husband had moved out of their home. As I listened and asked questions, it dawned on me that this woman's thinking was skewed. She would tell me one thing that happened between her husband and her, and then the next minute she would say, "But I will forgive him and things will work out." This was the pattern of our conversation for more than an hour. *How*, I wondered, *did this talented, intelligent Christian woman learn to live in a fantasy world? Who is telling her the truth about forgiveness?* I asked her, "Do you see what's wrong with what you're telling me? You think forgiving your husband will solve all your marriage problems, but that's not reality. You should forgive your husband, but you also need to accept that he's broken."

Then she said, "I don't want anyone to see us as broken." From the beginning of her marriage, this young woman had a warped perspective of forgiveness and reality.

When we recognize brokenness in relationships and our need to forgive, we are living in reality rather than framing the world as we wish it were. When we recognize that being in relationships with people means living in forgiveness, we are framing the world as it is. Forgiveness says, "You keep hurting me and our relationship is broken. I forgive you, but I'm changing my expectations of how we relate." This requires genuine effort and doesn't come easily.

Right thinking leads to right speaking, right living, and right relating—that's why it is important that we talk more openly about the challenges of forgiveness. Younger women need to learn how the Spirit of God leads them into all truth (John 16:13). God will give us exactly what we need in a situation. When we wait for him, we can open our hearts and ask him to help us live well with what is broken, with what's been taken from us, with where we may have sinned.

Are we willing to tell our daughters, our sisters, our nieces, our granddaughters, and the younger women around us the truth that we must forgive but that it doesn't always change the situation? I've become convinced that when we forgive with the awareness of this truth, we weaken the enemy's ability to keep us confused and distanced in our relationships.

Forgiveness Helps Us See the Bigger Picture

As we begin to understand forgiveness, we see that it cleans our hearts, is a choice, is ongoing, and doesn't always change the situation. God always sees the bigger picture and commands us to forgive for reasons we may never know. Obeying him in this area deeply affects our ministries, work, and family lives. This is true whether we are forgiving others or ourselves.

Scripture tells us:

- "Forgive, and you will be forgiven" (Luke 6:37).
- "If you forgive anyone's sins, their sins are forgiven; if you do not forgive them, they are not forgiven" (John 20:23).
- "For if you forgive other people when they sin against you, your heavenly Father will also forgive you" (Matt. 6:14).

When we forgive or are forgiven, our hearts become blameless and happy. God knew we might need to forgive more than seventy-seven times and be forgiven just as much (Matt. 18:22). In fact, when telling the parable of the unmerciful servant who was tortured for not forgiving a fellow servant, Jesus boldly said, "This is how my heavenly Father will treat each of you unless you forgive your brother or sister from your heart" (v. 35).

God sent Jesus to help us navigate relationships with others and our own selves. We are to: forgive and be forgiven, forgive and be happy, and forgive and be blameless. Happiness is a by-product of forgiveness, because joy runs free in a pure, blameless heart (Ps. 119:1).

Just as Christ saw his persecutors' hearts when he was on the cross and forgave them, saying, "Father, forgive them, for they do not know what they are doing" (Luke 23:34), when we forgive, it changes our hearts so that we can see the other person's humanity. My heart was changed when my mom told me more about her life and what it was like for her not to have a loving mother of her own. Through conversations like that, she would tell me how sorry she was for breaking up the family and leaving us. She was truly broken by her choices. I saw it in her tears; I heard it in her voice crumbling. Perhaps we are closest to Jesus when we choose to forgive.

Passing Along What We Know about Forgiveness

How forgiveness works is nothing short of a miracle. The results connect people, rebuild families, cement friendships, and support communities. It's absolutely worth every effort to keep our hearts clean.

If you've spent your adult years forgiving from your heart, then you are in a good place to help younger women do the same. Now that we've talked about the importance of knowing forgiveness, we need to consider how we can pass this along to the next generation. As you interact with women, you will discover they need your guidance in practicing the pattern of forgiveness. They need direction, through the power of the Holy Spirit, but also through you as you teach, model, and open up with them.

Here's what younger women need to know about living out this pattern and how you can guide them in practicing full forgiveness.

Full forgiveness gives freedom, silences the accuser's voice, softens our hearts, redeems situations, requires prayer, and believes God is at work.

Gives Freedom

Recently, I was having a hard time concentrating in prayer when I asked God what was holding me back. A little while later, I realized the obstruction was related to a woman who was demanding too much of me on a project. I stopped everything I was doing and called her. We worked it out, and I was once again eager about what I was doing. Freedom comes when we forgive.

You can help the younger women in your life identify whether they have truly forgiven someone or themselves by the evidence of freedom they are experiencing. For example, when appropriate, you can ask, "Have you taken the time to pray about the people in your life who you've felt hurt or shamed you?" Or you could describe the times you have felt choked or paralyzed in your spirit because you were holding something against someone.

Silences the Accuser's Voice

You can help others become more willing to forgive by helping them differentiate between the voice of the enemy and the voice of God. The enemy tries to keep us from being close to one another by not forgiving ourselves or others. He's behind the accusing voice in our heads:

- "She was never in favor of me, so why forgive her?"
- "She will never change. She's not worth forgiving."
- "I deserved to be treated that way because of who I am. I can never forgive myself."
- "I will make her suffer and hold on to vengeance."
- "I've sinned too many times. Jesus won't forgive me."

The accuser wants us to feel as if we're dressed in filthy clothes because then we'll live in shame. Women who feel shame often avoid getting close to others because they fear having their shame exposed.

But when we help a young woman recognize the accusing voices and discount them as lies or counter them with the truth, we strengthen her ability to follow God's command to forgive, which lessens the likelihood that she will live in shame. Forgiveness silences the accuser's voice in our heads and leads to encouragement.

Remember, Jesus died in order to forgive our sins—that is the meaning of salvation. We need to remind ourselves and others that if we do not believe that his children are blameless in his sight, shame and bitterness can turn us into miserable, intolerable women.

Softens Our Hearts

Recently, a young woman told me that she was done with a community group at her church. In the past, she had told me her frustrations with the way one woman treated her, and I talked to her about working these things out so she could stay in the group. But she pulled out and went into self-protection mode, where she became inflexible with her schedule and her life. When she informed me of her decision, I told her how in my own life when I forgave a person from my heart, I felt more gratitude for my other relationships because my heart was softened. The next time I saw her, her countenance had changed and she said, "I'm still going to meet with my group. I realized how not forgiving that one woman was keeping me from enjoying the benefits of all the women."

Redeems Situations

I once shared with a group of young professional women how a male colleague humiliated me when I was giving a talk to a group. In the middle of my talk, he stopped me and questioned where I had gotten my information. I knew I had worked hard researching the facts and said so. But afterward, I felt embarrassed that he had been so rude. However, if I had shut him down and shut him out, I would have had to live with a closed heart; so instead, I went to him and expressed how he had made me feel. A few days later, he found me and apologized because he had looked over all my research and seen it was accurate. He also admitted that he had felt intimidated by my hard work.

I told the women that story because I wanted to teach them healthy ways to deal with our hearts when we want to shut people down and shut people out. I wanted them to know that forgiveness offers people a chance to deal with their own stuff too, and when they do, the situations can be redeemed.

Requires Prayer

We can help young women understand what's going on in their hearts when a situation angers them or stirs them up in some way by praying with them about it. Being belittled by a boss or betrayed by a friend causes conflicting feelings of guilt and shame. When we offer to pray with someone who has been hurt, God's healing brings to light where forgiveness is needed.

Brad and I did this when a young couple called us one evening asking if we would come pray on their new property. A neighbor had filed a lawsuit against this couple before the property was to close. As the four of us stood holding hands, the young woman asked God to help her with her awful feelings toward this man who had no reason to file. As she prayed, I was reminded of God's promise that if we forgive, that person is forgiven. So together, we forgave this man aloud for his actions. Smiling, our friend said, "Thank you. I wanted to delay the process of forgiving him, but when you prayed, I felt my heart soften and a compassion trumped my anger." Four days later, the man dropped the lawsuit. In this case, forgiveness did seem to change the circumstances!

Believes God Is at Work

As I said earlier, many women are facing serious issues that are causing them pain and confusion—from discovering their husbands are living double lives, to raising children on their own, to facing financial loss, to experiencing clinical depression and battling thoughts of suicide. They need our help in finding hope, and oftentimes this means learning to forgive.

A good question to ask in these times is, "Can you articulate what you need from God in this circumstance?" or "How have you seen God work even in the small details lately?" These kinds of open questions can help them see God's activity in their lives. During intense, stressful times, it's not helpful to ask, "How did you get to such a bad place?" Our dependence on the Holy Spirit is what we need more than anything to support young women in the belief that God is at work on their behalf.

A fundamental reality about life is that people and circumstances will create stress and disappointment. As one person said, "The inability to address problems is what complicates life." Time, careers, children, illness, and age all bring new circumstances where we will need to forgive. I have to remind myself regularly, even daily, that my goal in relationships is restoration—anger, resentment, hardness, and disappointment will not help anyone grow in

God's grace. As Brad sometimes tells me, "You don't need to always be right. Let it go."

Never stop knowing the results of full forgiveness.

Glimpses of Wholeness

Even though I practiced forgiving my mom and myself for my sinful reactions to her, I held back from my mother for years. It hurt too much to love her with all my heart. I wanted to, but my first instinct was always to protect my heart. I also attempted to fix what went wrong until I realized that I couldn't. It wasn't until I was in my thirties that I understood that during all those interactions with my mother, God was with me, vying for my attention. He knew that as my mother and I fumbled with our roles of mother and daughter, both of us would end up carrying the blame, the guilt, and the shame.

As I accepted that forgiveness is a process, God redeemed parts of our relationship. Ironically, when I worked hard at forgiving myself for hardening my heart toward my mother, God gave me glimpses of wholeness on this side of eternity.

Late one cold December night, the night before my mom was to fly back to Philadelphia after a week in Oregon, the Spirit of God impressed on me to pray for her. We often prayed together during our visits, but this time was different. The sense I had was that God wanted to give my mom something new. We had had a fight earlier that day in a restaurant—even the waitress had gotten involved—and my attitude was not one of prayer. I was convinced that because of our words, my mom wouldn't want me to pray for her or with her.

But I walked into the guest room and asked, "Mom, do you want to pray before you leave?"

Instantly, she said, "Yes, let's do it now."

The moment I placed my hand on her shoulder, I prayed for her with deep and precious words of encouragement. I was just the channel for a loving Father to tell his daughter that it was a new day. My mom's spirit softened, and her face shone as she received more of the Holy Spirit through prayer; it wasn't the result of intellectual thoughts of positive energy. Heaven came down and visited us. It was the closest I had ever felt to my mother. In that intersection of mercy and guilt, I was compelled to love and speak truth with the whole of my heart. My mom prayed for me too, seeing me as whole, not as one who was damaged by her actions. We shared a genuine love for each other. I know in heaven that we will share a whole and healthy mother and daughter relationship. For now, we are given glimpses of what that can be like.

The days Mom and I are transparent about the accuser's voice in our heads are some of our best days. I'm given the chance to say, "Mom, we can't turn back time and change what happened, but the truth is, you are forgiven in God's sight. Please don't let the guilt rob you of joy in your three adult children and five grandchildren. I forgive you." And when I openly tell her about the voice of rejection I can still hear at times, she says to me, "Pam, I love you and I want to be with you." In those vulnerable moments, I hear the words of a powerful promise that keeps my heart open: "He will never leave you nor forsake you" (Deut. 31:6).

Forgiveness is a way to know the truth rather than fantasy; it's a form of protection rather than self-protection. As we open our hearts to obey God in forgiving ourselves and others, his Spirit ministers to the world around us because nothing is more beautiful than a free, happy heart. And it's in our free, happy, *forgiven* hearts that the women in our lives will catch glimpses of our holy God.

Chapter Seven

Relating with Compassion

It is in the shelter of each other that the people live.

Gaelic proverb

In Genesis we read the story of how Joseph, beloved by his father, was betrayed by his brothers, thrown into a pit, and sold as a slave. Scripture tells us he was sold again later to a man named Potiphar and that "the LORD was with Joseph" (Gen. 39:2) and gave him success managing Potiphar's household. Later, when Joseph was thrown into prison after Potiphar's wife falsely accused him of trying to seduce her, God was with him again (v. 21), and the keeper of the prison put Joseph in charge of the prisoners. God gave Joseph the supernatural ability to interpret dreams, and because of this gift he gained the attention of Pharaoh. When Joseph interpreted a dream for Pharaoh that no one else had been able to decipher, Pharaoh made Joseph the second most powerful person in Egypt.

Joseph's life is an example of God's providential care in the extremes. Just as quickly as he was thrown into pits and prisons, he was promoted and became successful and well loved. The narrator said, "But the LORD was with Joseph and showed him steadfast love and gave him favor" (Gen. 39:21 ESV). "God was with him and rescued him out of all his afflictions and gave him favor and wisdom before Pharaoh" (Acts 7:9–10 ESV).

It's in this context that Joseph recognized his brothers when they came to Egypt to buy food because of a famine; his brothers, however, did not recognize him. He accused them of being spies and said one of them needed to stay in Egypt in prison while the others went home and returned with their youngest brother, so that Joseph would know they had been telling him the truth about who they were. Later, Joseph overheard the brothers talking, distressed and fearful that this suffering had come to them as punishment for what they had done to him.

When he first saw his youngest brother, Benjamin, Joseph was not prepared for the depth of emotion he would feel (Gen. 43:29–30). His compassion for Benjamin was so strong, he removed himself from his brothers' presence.

In his private room, Joseph wept. When he had collected himself, he invited them to dinner and they "feasted and drank freely with him" (v. 34).

Joseph was not quite ready to reveal himself to his brothers, though. As they were getting ready to return home, he told his steward to fill their sacks with food and money and also to put his silver cup in Benjamin's sack. After the brothers left, Joseph sent his steward after them to search for the cup. The brothers proclaimed their innocence and agreed that if the steward found the cup in one of their sacks, then the brother who had the cup would become Joseph's slave. When the cup was found in Benjamin's sack, the brothers were horrified to think of what it would do to their father to lose another son. When they were brought before Joseph, the oldest brother, Judah, pleaded with Joseph to let him take Benjamin's place.

What was going through Joseph's mind at that moment? Perhaps he was thinking, *I see my mother in my younger brother's eyes. I want to protect him. I want to know him.* Or perhaps he was thinking of how his father had loved him and how painful it must have been for him to believe that Joseph was dead. And perhaps when Joseph was standing before Benjamin and his other brothers he recognized that he was fully capable of the same rotten things they had done.

While we don't know what was going on in Joseph's mind at the time, we do know that God's compassion welled up within him. The gold Joseph received from his suffering with God was in becoming intimately aware of divine tenderness. And when his heart swelled in tenderness for his brothers, it forced Joseph to move into the room of decision. Would he choose to demonstrate God's compassion and extend grace to his family, or would he choose to withhold it?

Joseph chose compassion. Unable to control his emotions any longer, he made himself known to them with loud weeping (Gen. 45:1–2). His grace and compassion united his family—a family marred by deceit, jealousy, and hatred. Joseph confirmed that God's eternal purpose for the things he had suffered was the "saving of many lives" (50:20). Then he said and did something that could have come only from the Holy Spirit—he told his brothers not to be afraid and he would provide for them: "He reassured them and spoke kindly to them" (v. 21). It wasn't a trite speech where he was initiating all this good to meet his abandonment needs. He did everything possible to bring his brothers close to him. Compassion holds people close.

God's hand was on Joseph because he followed God's ways and chose to forgive those who had hurt him. God gave him compassion, but it was up to Joseph to decide if he wanted to express it or not. That's what the room of decision is for. Joseph is an extraordinary example of someone who related with compassion toward people who treated him despicably and wanted him dead. He was close to God, and God protected him when others sought to harm him. His compassionate response to his brothers saved them—and it saved the entire Israelite nation.[1]

When we come face-to-face with betrayal—as Joseph did—or hate, fear, despair, depression, or darkness, our compassionate responses can help save the next generation.

Compassion Defined

If understanding (see chapter 5) requires us to *do* something when a young woman is at a crossroads, then compassion pleads with us to *be* something, no matter if that person has hurt or disappointed us, disagrees with our theological point of view, or is someone to whom we can barely relate. Expressed compassion is the result of our having said yes to God one million times along the way. Joseph did this, and that was why he was able to choose compassion in the face of his brothers' betrayal.

Compassion is not the same as sympathy. Sympathy is feeling sorry for what happened to a person; compassion steps into what happened. Henri Nouwen, author and Catholic priest, offered an amazing definition of *compassion*:

> The word *compassion* is derived from the Latin words *pati* and *cum*, which together mean "to suffer with." Compassion asks us to go where it hurts, to enter into places of pain, to share in brokenness, fear and confusion and anguish. Compassion challenges us to cry out with those in misery, to mourn with those who are lonely, to weep with those in tears. Compassion requires us to be weak with the weak, vulnerable with the vulnerable, and powerless with the powerless. Compassion means full immersion in the condition of being human.[2]

Compassion doesn't judge how a woman found herself in an awful situation, nor does it think, *I'm glad I'm not going through what she's going through!* Compassion does not analyze or criticize. It says, "I feel what you feel"; it comes alongside another person and puts itself in her place.

Why We Need Compassion

I've learned that in order for a person to feel safe enough to admit she's done something wrong or is in a horrible place because of someone else's destructiveness, she must first be treated with compassion. A woman speaks her true heart, no matter the condition, when she's given compassion.

When the women in our lives suffer from clinical depression or the death of a loved one, we must have the compassionate heart of our heavenly Father, no matter what it costs us. When a woman says she was raped or confesses she's in an abusive relationship, we cannot stand in judgment or indifference or shock. Such uncompassionate responses put a distance between us and make her feel far away from God.

I know several young women who are suffering from a void of a loving church community and meaningful involvement. They need other women to come alongside them, to feel what they feel, to walk in their shoes, so they can settle down into knowing God cares about them. It doesn't help to ask them, "Well, have you checked out all the churches in the area?" These women need compassion; they need someone to ask, "What happened with your last church experience?"

When we come face-to-face with a young woman who was the victim of sex trafficking, or who is fighting cancer, or whose husband has just died and left her to support and raise two small children, we must show compassion. We must let our hearts feel deeply, cry with them as they share their stories, and listen before moving on to the next thing. We must become human. Sometimes, the best way to show compassion is to be fully present to the person's pain. "I'm so, so sorry. What are you experiencing? Please tell me. I want to hear your heart."

When we face despair, depression, and darkness as our young friend discovers her new baby will never walk and most likely will never talk and have a normal life, we must live out the compassion that God has given to us and not let fear keep us away. The greater the sacrifice required of us, the more God gives us his heart. The more we depend on God's Spirit for how to respond to the people and circumstances in our lives, rather than depending on our own emotional reactions, the more compassion we are able to pour into another's life. This is what it means to walk in the Spirit.

It is not easy to stop relying on our own hearts. It requires us to sacrifice our natural inclinations, but when we do, God pours into us the compassion of Jesus Christ and we have the potential to remove the feeling of distance between another woman and God. Compassion has the potential to shift something inside her, inviting more openness for God to come in and heal. Imagine, for a moment, how a compassionate response might affect a young woman who tells you, as one woman told me, that she has an eating disorder that preoccupies her entire inner life, reminding her constantly how she must "disappoint God."

It doesn't matter if you naturally feel compassion or if you are naturally uncompassionate, because God can change your heart so that it is more like his. He can give you his compassion, so that you in turn can pour it onto others. When you relate to the women in your life with the Father's compassion, you show them his face and give them a clearer picture of who he is—tender and warm and kind. For one woman, it could mean she chooses to live her life in God. For another, it could mean throwing herself into his loving arms for the first time. For many young women, it could give them the strength, hope, and courage they need to feel safe and protected in their faith, reminding them in that moment that they are not lost but found. There's not a circumstance on the face of this earth where God's compassion cannot reach—nothing and no one are hidden from his sight.

Living Out the Heart of Compassion

One day last January, I received a text from a woman I care deeply about that sent my spirit spinning. She had had an affair.

A Christian who prays and is prayed for regularly, this woman is committed in her faith and loves God with all her heart. It was her deepest desire to make her marriage whole and healthy. I'd prayed for her, her family, and her children for many years. Long-distance phone calls and yearly visits kept us close. With so much emotional and spiritual investment from myself and others, I was hopeful God would move heaven and earth to bring love and joy and life to this marriage.

When I heard the situation had gone from bad to worse, despair enveloped me. A thousand feelings ran through my heart; compassion was not one of them. What I wanted to do was board a plane, drive to where she was, pack her bags, gather her children, and take her back to her husband. Instead, as soon as I read the text, I did the next thing.

Worship, Don't Wallow

I taught my writing classes early that morning, and rather than head to the library as usual, I drove to a local church, longing for the anointed room called the sanctuary. I sat at the piano and worshiped, tears streaming down my face. I felt far away from this woman and from God. Finding it difficult to concentrate or express the depth of how I felt for her and her family and what she must have been facing, I stood up and walked over to the front pew.

With pen and paper in hand, I captured these words as they fell from heaven:

I've been climbing the stairs of loneliness,
leading me nowhere near your loveliness,
Looking past the highest step, past the farthest star,
Staring straight into the night,
worshiping from afar,
I cry out into the darkness with
no answer in my heart,
Leaning further over wondering
How grief's sadness followed me this far
But then a Voice behind me
said, "Walk in this way."
I turned my heart, I turned my soul, as the
distance between us vanished to gray
I spoke your name, Jesus
The powers of darkness gone
I cried your name, Savior
The longing became my song
Hold me
Hold me close
Hold me closer, still
With the brilliance of his glory, his
Presence covered my story.
Like the Father, is the Son—their
holy love is making me one.
He anoints me with highest joy,
Sustains me with most powerful words
No one is like the Heir; nothing
in earth or heaven compares

And now that Voice is in me
saying, "All I have is yours."
I hear all the angels singing, "Let
the Holy Spirit pour."
I spoke your name, Jesus
The powers of darkness gone
I cried your name, Savior
The longing became my song
Hold me
Hold me close.*

Somehow when I worshiped with my heart full of grief, God filled me with compassion for my friend. I believe that his compassion for her and her broken family was so deep that he gave me words to fill the spaces where judgment or condemnation would naturally dwell. Welling up inside me was God's tender compassion for her rather than my natural feelings of being appalled. The human heart cries out, "Hold me," and the compassion of God's heart does just that—it holds us to him and to one another. When I did eventually talk to my friend that day or the next, I wasn't detached or angry or accusing. Instead, I simply listened as she talked about why she had done what she had done. I heard what she had to say without trying to fix her situation. But I would not have been able to do that if I had not first spent some time with God in worship.

---

* To download "Hold Me Close," go to www.pamelalau.com/song. Lyrics by Pam Lau. Music by Olivia Pothoff.

Come Alongside, Not Above

The day I wrote the song and talked to my friend on the phone, I came alongside her as a compassionate soul, not a condemning woman. I listened anew as she told me her story.

As a woman who didn't understand her own value, my friend excessively guarded her heart in relationships with some men and was foolishly vulnerable with others. She wanted unconditional love but sought it in an abusive relationship that characterized her eight-year marriage. When she got married, she knew she was compromising herself, and because she didn't seek God for her worth, her despair only increased. She believed that through submitting to the man she had married, she would be valued and ultimately find the security she had longed for since she was a little girl. She allowed herself to be used as a sexual object, despite the lack of emotional intimacy with her husband. She allowed herself to be controlled and manipulated, simply because she was afraid to lose "love." It was from this place of being shattered and longing for love that she sought wholeness in the arms of another man.

That day on the phone, I asked her why she had had the affair, and she said that the other man made her "feel incredibly loved and deeply valued. He heard my heart and accepted me despite my darkest confessions." She explained how she had tried to reconcile her marriage even though she loved this man. "I left the man I loved in an attempt to reconcile my marriage only to be mentally and verbally abused; unfortunately, I stayed because I thought I deserved it."

So there we were on the phone, steeped in the whole story with its mess and consequences, with its tangled webs and raw confessions. And somehow what started rising within me was a warm and tender compassion for this woman whose lifelong search for value had landed her in a desperate place. I felt the tenderness of God pour from my heart for my friend. Rather than cut her decisions into pieces, I saw her as a little girl longing to be valued, I wept with her as she told me stories of her abusive husband, and I became weak as she was weak, vulnerable as she was vulnerable. And then I kindly asked, "Where do we go from here?"

Feel—Don't Be Afraid to Be Deeply Moved

What I've learned is that when we cry out to God from the pain of those he brings to us, he cries with us. But we need to feel, to take the time to feel deeply. When we do, compassion takes root in our character and we are transformed more into the character of God.

When this woman is in my presence and reveals her true self, I weep for her out of love for her. Isn't that how God describes his own heart toward his people in the Scriptures? "I led them with cords of kindness, with the bands of love, and I became to them as one who eases the yoke on their jaws, and I bent down to them and fed them" (Hosea 11:4 ESV). Our relationship with God is always rooted in his redemptive love. He truly feels tender and loving toward us. When we take the time to feel deeply moved by another person's suffering, we too show a tender love.

Hold On to the Helper

How can we continue staying close to others when our own perspectives blind us? When my friend first texted me about her decision to leave her marriage, my initial response was to try to put her life back together the way I thought it should look. I did not know about the abuse she had experienced; all I could see was that she was destroying her family through divorce. But if I'd done that, if I had gone into striving mode, I would have pushed her away from me. I would have put distance between us.

But because I held on to the Holy Spirit, he was able to break through my initial response and show me what was behind my reaction. As the Holy Spirit moved closer to me and formed pictures in my mind, I saw the "boulders" that kept me from being deeply touched by her story: I saw the resentment I felt about another stable family falling apart and its effect on all of us, and I pushed it aside. I saw the fear that, despite being happily married, I too might someday be vulnerable to the attentions of another man, and I pushed that boulder aside. I began to pray that God would open my heart to whatever he had for me as he revealed each boulder.

Of course, I knew my friend's history in part, but hearing it this time, I experienced it differently. I let her story change me as I listened. I was fully engaged with her and became one with her story. All the while, I held on to the Helper. I realized that I needed to be careful not to be "god" in this woman's life. It's the Spirit's place to change, to convict, to lead. My job was to come alongside.

While my friend was telling me her story, I tried to have one ear tuned in to her and what she was saying and the other to Christ and what his Spirit was telling me. As I did, he began to convict me about my self-righteous attitude. Who was I to point my finger at her for having an affair? Were my battles with control and fear sins that fell into different categories? Didn't I seek value in projects that made me feel important? Humbled by the work God was doing in my own heart, I confessed how every day these attitudes block the compassionate heart of God in my life for another person. The Spirit showed me that each day I'm one breath away from doing something that could destroy my own family.

Sacrifice

My friend, like everyone in need of compassion, was struggling to feel Christ's presence in her life. She knew that her decision to escape the pain of her marriage by having an affair was wrong, and her guilt created distance between her and God. By treating her with compassion instead of judgment, I was sacrificing my agenda for her life to look a certain way. It was a sacrifice for her to admit her desires were wrong. And when she did, at the lowest point, she experienced God's compassionate love.

There's a story about John, the gospel writer, that is well-known from the writings of the Jewish historian Josephus. John pastored a small church and mentored a young man. Years later when he returned to see how his church was doing, he asked about the young man. The bishop explained that the young man had backslid and left the faith. Immediately, John requested a horse and rider to find the young man. John traveled to the town and discovered that the young man had returned to drinking and stealing. John pleaded with him to return with him. The answer was no. Finally, John fell to his knees and begged the young man to return to the faith. Unable to refuse, the young man agreed, and through John's pastoral care, he was restored to the church and to his faith.

In this story John and the young man each had to make a sacrifice. John had to sacrifice his schedule and time to find the young man. Further, he had to sacrifice his own agenda for how he expected this young man's life to look. Without an agenda, he was unhindered to do what mattered most: move into the room of decision and reveal the heart of God. Compassion compelled John to act.

The young man had to sacrifice his natural desire to please himself. God's compassion as seen through John compelled him to wrench himself away from his desires. John recognized the sacrifice it took for this young man and nurtured him back to life in God.

When it comes to your relationships, you too may be asked to make a sacrifice of time or an agenda in order to give compassion. I'm not advocating for you to ignore the healthy boundaries God has taught you through the years. All of us have situations in our lives where compassion is desperately needed. I know it's painful to invest in others and then not have anything to show for it. Or we just don't know how to get ourselves in that woman's presence so we can show the heart of God.

Here's what I want you to take from this: Whenever God makes you aware of a younger woman in need of compassion, remember your years with him and worship, letting God hold you close. As he pours out his compassion on you, make the decision to pour out the last drop on the soul in need. Reassure the woman who is suffering, sacrifice your own agenda, and speak kindly to her. Your compassion for the next generation could be the "saving of many lives."

Chapter Eight

Conversations about Sex

Although it is true that having sex can turn a student
away from worship, from faith, even from God—it
also seems that these shifts can be reversed. Moreover,
the shared campus culture at evangelical schools
tends to keep sex and the soul in conversation.

Donna Freitas, *Sex and the Soul*

The evening begins with the sound of a doorbell at 9:00 p.m. in a Seattle home. A young couple walks through the door for a personal conversation that they've never had with anyone else. The hosts, Kate and Kyle, offer them something to drink, making them feel at home. Light music plays in the background. The recently married couple have come for help regarding an issue that would impact their marriage. The couples face each other on comfortable chairs as the young man speaks, "The other night I told Sarah I've struggled with looking at porn for six years. When I was thirteen, I used porn when I was stressed. Now I don't know if I can stop."

Sarah hangs her head as her husband admits his addiction. When she speaks, it is to confess that she has doubts about whether she is pretty enough to make him stop. She asks, "As we keep having sex, will his need for porn change? Will I ever be enough? I even had him show it to me and now I'm furious."

Kate understands that Sarah is thinking, *Our sex and love are dirty and tainted; this means I am too.* Kate says, "Sarah, I want you to know that this isn't about you fulfilling Joel's broken desires. When Kyle first told me he looked at porn, I thought it was because I lacked something. But then a wise woman helped me to realize it wasn't about me, that it was about sexual addiction. I decided to make this journey of Kyle's healing and our marriage a lifelong commitment. Kyle isn't addicted to porn anymore, but he does have his occasional setbacks. He has learned to be honest with me about when he is feeling tempted and also when he looks at a movie or website he shouldn't. He's asked me and a group of friends to hold him accountable."

Kate and Kyle lead small group discussions with engaged and married couples who are struggling with sexual issues, especially pornography. Kate and Kyle are helping hundreds of couples work through this issue together by teaching them to recognize the problem and to communicate openly with each other about their desires to be whole in their sexuality.

I've stopped being shocked by the number of men who use pornography and by their stories of how young they were when it entered their hearts. After all, pornography is easily accessed on the Internet. Gone are the days of brown-paper-covered magazines secretly mailed to viewers once a month. While sexually explicit computer images of naked women arouse and entrap our men, sex scenes in the form of entertaining literature are capturing the minds and hearts of our women.

Fifty Shades of Grey, a 2011 erotic romance novel by British author E. L. James, has topped bestseller lists around the world, including the United States, and produced two sequels. Notable for its explicitly erotic scenes featuring bondage/discipline, dominance/submission, and sadism/masochism, the series has sold more than one hundred million copies worldwide and been translated into fifty-two languages, setting the record for the fastest-selling paperback of all time.

I find it disturbing that many women, including Christian women, claim that these books have improved their sex lives. I can guarantee none of us would want the young women we know to be sexually involved with *Fifty*'s main character, Christian Grey. But I wouldn't want the young women I know to be ignorant of the problems that come when men have an addiction to pornography, either.

It's a Different World

We are in the midst of another sexual shift in society, and many Christians are following the culture right on cue. Rather than rethinking what the role of sex should be in their lives, many believers are accepting the world's standards and mimicking the sexual practices of their peers and what's portrayed in media.

Let me ask you: How should the church respond to the obsession of sex in our culture? I believe that if we don't want to let E. L.

James have the most influence over how young women view sex, then it is critical that those of us who are married begin having explicit conversations about sex with younger Christian women. We don't do them any favors when we ignore these matters and fail to talk with them about their questions and concerns or about what is happening in the culture at large. We are doing them a great disservice when we don't gently and firmly tell them the truth about sexual intimacy and related issues.

I want to persuade you to find the courage to start talking openly with the women around you about sexual issues they may encounter and to communicate truth to them. If you are willing to be that person, then keep reading.

Attitudes and views about sex have shifted in our society; even if we don't agree with the changes, we must know the sexual realities in which our young women live. They are engaging in behaviors without examining them through the lens of Scripture, including living together without a commitment, embracing the gay lifestyle, viewing porn, and engaging in casual sex. On the opposite end of the cultural spectrum is the emphasis in some Christian circles on purity rings. While this idea may sound Christian, it has no grounding in Scripture. We cannot have discussions about such things apart from what Scripture teaches; however, we cannot have these discussions apart from culture, either. I want your voice to be so powerful in the lives of the young women that the voices of culture are not the only ones calling out for vulnerability. Tell women with your words and actions that they have a friend in you, that you love and care for them very much, and that it is safe for them to share with you their "deepest, darkest, sickest parts."[1]

Problematic Messages

In talking with young women, I've identified several messages they have been receiving that are contributing to the problems some are having in the areas of sex and sexuality.

A Nun before Marriage, a Sex Goddess during Marriage

Some Christians send young women a message that says they should abstain from sex and its dangerous, mysterious power until marriage, but then, after getting married, they are to become sexual goddesses and to love everything about sex twenty-four-seven. This idea is even more entrenched in the hearts of young women who have taken part in the "purity ring–wait until marriage" vows that have become popular with some Christian families and youth movements around the country.

We need to tell young women that sex is a beautiful and fun experience but that it's best to wait for marriage. Further, we need to open up in our conversations about the actual act of sex, how it works, and why it might be painful. Young women need to know these things before they get married. We need to explain that good sex rarely happens the first time two virgins are on a honeymoon. And that's okay.

Tori came back from her honeymoon livid. Chastity, purity, "wait until marriage" messages had been preached to her all her life. She was raised in a Christian home where most topics were discussed openly—except the topic of sex. After graduating from a public school, Tori attended a Christian university where she attended chapel services a few times a week. When the chapel speakers did mention sex, it was always in the context of saving sex for marriage.

The months leading up to their wedding day were stressful yet exciting. It was getting more difficult to remain "pure" the closer she and Clay grew in their relationship. Tori knew the facts about the birds and the bees, but no one had ever sat down with her and talked with her about what to expect when making love with her husband for the first time. But she wasn't worried about her lack of knowledge. She reasoned that since she had such a strong desire for sex, she and Clay could figure it out. They both wanted to wait to make their first sexual experience special, romantic, and right before God. That commitment, she reasoned, deserved God's blessing.

On her honeymoon, Tori had a panic attack because her first sexual intimate encounter with Clay was a disaster. The two of them stumbled around, awkwardly taking their clothes off, and when she and Clay tried to have sex, neither was physically ready and it was deeply frustrating and embarrassing for both of them. Tori wondered, *Was it this awkward for everyone the first time they made love—or just for me and Clay?* Every night of their honeymoon was a repeat performance of the first night. This was heartbreaking for both of them. They both felt like failures.

While the idea of saving sex for marriage is good, it is not enough simply to teach abstinence. It's not enough to preach to our young women, "Don't have sex until you're married." Tori needed to be told something like this: "You might not like sex the first few times; it can be awkward and you could feel like your husband is being selfish. You might not experience an orgasm right away. Do you know what that is? Sex is about giving pleasure and it takes time to figure out what someone wants. I'm in full support of saving sex until marriage, but I want you to know you can ask me anything you want to know!"

A Free-for-All Sexual Lifestyle Is Healthy and Normal

Another troublesome message says that a woman's body is a sexual object and that the most important thing about a woman is that she is a sexual being. Television shows and movies portray sexual activity as the norm for not just young adults but even for high school students. In magazines and advertisements the female body is typically presented through a sex-gratifying lens. The message sent is that it is normal and healthy for single women to engage in a free-for-all sexual lifestyle and that they can do so without negative consequences. Media don't show the percentages of young women who have sexually transmitted diseases, unplanned pregnancies, shattered hearts, and sexual problems later on when they are married. How might the inner lives of our young women be transformed if media portrayed the reality that every time a woman has sex with someone, she gives a piece of her soul away?

Let me assure you: our young Christian women are absolutely influenced by this message. They claim, however, that even though they know having sexual intimacy outside of marriage is wrong, they do not know the reasons why it is wrong because they have never been told. Many feel that the Christian message about sex is not compelling enough to help them "endure" waiting until they get married. Sure, they want to please God, but they want to be convinced—lovingly, that is.

I met Shanna through a mutual friend and we instantly discovered our similar interest in good books. We got together several times over coffee and often swapped our latest reads. One time while we were dialoguing about a spiritual issue of a character in a book we had both read, Shanna, who is not married, confessed to me how she desperately wanted to be close to God but that she knew she'd done something wrong. Surprised by the turn of conversation, I listened more carefully and asked her what she thought she had done wrong.

Ranking it as the "worst" sin, she told me she had had sex with a guy because she had been tired of waiting and just wanted to be close to someone. "I wasn't just trying to get some action; I was longing for intimacy, vulnerability, to feel loved." I asked her if she was still with this guy and she said, "No. I never wanted to marry him. I just wanted to be close to him." I asked her if she was feeling lonely and without friends. Shanna shook her head and said, "Yes and no. I have women friends and I feel close to my mom and grandmother. But they live thousands of miles away. I just didn't think having sex would be a big deal—it happens all the time in movies! But no one prepared me for the heartache." Shanna explained that she felt like pieces of her were given away every time she had sex.

Instead of just hoping and praying that the young women in our lives will wait until marriage to have sex, we need to get over our discomfort so that we can have frank conversations with them about their questions and their sexual experiences and the pressures they may be experiencing. They need and want women to help them with their second-guessing and guilt when it comes to sexual issues, intimacy, and identity.

Both Tori and Shanna are missing important pieces of what God has to say about sex. Somehow you and I must communicate these truths, in a spirit of love, when talking with younger women about sex and sexuality. We need to help women understand God's ways when it comes to our sexuality so they can make good decisions and, more important, know why they are making those decisions.

What We Say and Teach about Sex

Let me be clear: I'm not asking you to *initiate* conversations about sexual issues and relationships. However, the more time you spend with a young woman, the more comfortable she will feel in sharing her deeper thoughts, feelings, and concerns about sex. If she feels safe with you, she won't hold back, and she won't want you to hold back from her, either. She will start the conversation as she feels closer to you. But keep in mind that she may feel a lot of shame around her sexual identity. Focus on Christ's identity in her and her identity in Christ so he can transform the shame to freedom and joy.

That being said, here are some key truths about sex that young women need to know.

Why Abstinence before Marriage Is Important

1. The Bible confines sex to marriage. When talking with women about sex, I take care to communicate that married sex can be a good, spiritual experience. According to Scripture, God wants us to experience this spiritual union with one person; that's his preference.[2] Because the enemy has deceived an entire generation into thinking that casual sex does not impact our closeness with God or with others, it's our responsibility to say something about it. Young people need to know that it's sin when we are sexually intimate with people who are not our spouses. We say these things in the context of a loving conversation.

2. Sex affects our hearts. Having sex with other people affects more than our physical bodies; sex touches our inward selves. Because the heart is deceitful above all else, sin can turn sex into an idol. Sexual intimacy is something we do and experience wholeheartedly; it requires all of our being. Unless sex is for giving of one's self, it becomes very distorted, and sexual sin affects our hearts differently than other sins do.[3]

3. Sex unites two people. When two people have sex, they become one with each other. If I understand Scripture rightly—I'm a journalist, not a Bible scholar—then every person's deepest desire is to be one with someone.[4] We crave union. What does that mean? It means that sex is a uniting experience that we long for and is somehow a taste of eternity. We will know this oneness every moment we are in Jesus's presence in heaven. The longings we have for sex, even our corrupted longings, stem from this God-created desire to be one with another person.

This begs the question: Why would we want to give ourselves over to a unifying experience with someone if we are not one in every other area of life? That's a good question to ask our younger friends when they are torn between their sexual desires and their need for commitment.

Sex Is Not Dirty

Young women also need to understand that sexual desire is not a sin, nor is hot married sex. A lot of Christian women think that sexual desire is a bad thing. It's our responsibility to help them navigate their shameful feelings so they don't believe this lie. They need to know that sex is good and even spiritual. When I talk about marital sex with the younger women in my life, I speak to them as if they were my own daughters. I would never want my daughters to hear me portray sex as anything other than beautiful, fun, freeing, and with my own husband.

I smiled when Emily, a married woman in her midthirties, said she just didn't feel sexy anymore and wondered what she could do to spice things up a bit when making love to her husband.

"Initiate more sex," I said.

Emily blushed and said, "How do I do that?"

I did with Emily what I will do with my daughters when they are ready: I drove her to Victoria's Secret and we laughed for two hours in the dressing rooms. She tells me things are heating up a bit more in her bedroom.

Sex Can Be Disciplined

It is possible to control our sexual desires when certain support systems are in place. In our sex-saturated culture, it's important to find like-minded individuals or couples who believe sex doesn't control us. Whether we are single or married, if we struggle with the guidelines Scripture teaches, then we need community to help us stay committed. I know several women who meet regularly with younger women for the sole purpose of accountability in sexual activity. The older women tell me it's not easy to hear, but they know their presence is helping the young women reach their goals.

Identity Is Not Connected to Purity or Holiness

Our most powerful identity is our identity in Christ[5]—that's what our message should be. A woman's sexual purity, sexual impurities, or sexual orientation (if she says she's lesbian or straight or bi or transgender) is not her number one identity. A disconnect happens for young women when the church talks about a woman's sexuality as her identity. This happens as Christians encourage sexual purity but leave out crucial information. When we make the main message that a woman should guard her purity, if she then she loses it, she often identifies herself as less valuable. What about girls and young women who have been sexually abused or are already having sex? Once something happens to them sexually, they now identify themselves as unholy and impure. They see themselves as unclean.

We also misplace a woman's identity when we focus too much on her outward appearance and the way she dresses because we assume she's sexually active or wants to be.

Pay attention to what you are saying. The goal is to focus on Jesus Christ as our true identity. Any other identity shuts women off because they know they will never be good enough, never dress quite right, never attract the right kind of attention. In Jesus Christ they will find wholeness and healing—and our most powerful identity is to see ourselves in him.

What to Expect That First Night

If a young woman has abstained from sex until marriage, she needs to have realistic expectations of the first night. Many young women expect they will be having sex all night long on their honeymoon. After all, some songs actually say that's what's happening! In reality, the groom often ejaculates before they even have sex. This happens because he has not trained his body to hold back. A virgin may not enjoy lovemaking initially because she isn't able to have an orgasm and doesn't understand the mechanics for how to achieve sexual climax. You might not need to say it that bluntly—you don't want to make her afraid of her first night! It's best to use discernment as you share this information. But for many well-educated young women, they want to know the reality of what to expect.

Be prepared to tell young women that with good communication, monogamous sex gets better over time.

Sexual Concerns That May Come Up in Conversation

What might you expect to hear if a young woman brings up the topic of sexual problems? Here is a sampling of the kinds of issues you might encounter, how they usually make young women feel, and what is important for you to communicate in your conversations about these problems.

Pornography

When a young woman discovers her boyfriend or husband is using porn, she immediately feels as though she is not enough. What she needs to hear from you is that using porn is not good for a healthy relationship and that the addiction has nothing to do with her. Encourage her to get a pastor involved with her boyfriend or husband so he can receive some counseling. Help her to see she doesn't have to end the relationship but she cannot keep secrets about the porn. Connecting to a community (like the one described in the beginning of this chapter) and getting help are key.

Sex without Commitment

If a young, unmarried woman tells you she is having sex, she's likely having it a couple of times a week. Because she knows the Bible says sex outside of marriage is wrong, she feels like a failure. She also feels isolated and alone because her shame keeps her from talking to anyone else about what she is doing. On the other hand, she likes having sex and says it makes her feel closer to her partner. She may tell you she feels addicted to the sex because even though she wants to stop having it, she can't seem to stop herself.

So what does she need from you? A woman who is having sex without commitment needs someone to listen to her and to tell her she's not tainted. Be prepared to remind her of her identity, who she is in God's eyes: worthy.[6] Talk about who God calls her to be—his beloved, his daughter[7]—within that first conversation. Wait until the second or third conversation to mention how sex is meant for marriage. She already knows that or she wouldn't be talking about it with you. She's brought it up because she feels safe and trusts you won't add to her shame.

Masturbation

Normally, people don't talk about masturbation. I'm not comfortable talking about it, but if I can write about it, I'm confident you can talk about it in conversation. Here's what you need to know:[8]

- Masturbation doesn't have to do with wanting sex but wanting to control something in life when nothing else feels as if it can be controlled. It's a form of relaxation for some women who feel stressed or as if life is getting out of control.

- When a young woman shares with you that she is masturbating and feels ashamed, it's because she's kept it a secret. The best thing you can say to her is "It's not dirty; it's not something you are doing wrong."

- Some struggle with it as an addiction because they depend on masturbating to achieve climax several times a day. They shouldn't feel shame, but they should pay attention to how they're living if masturbating goes beyond normal limits. Tell them they need to talk to a professional counselor to find out the reason behind their behaviors.

- Some young women don't know that what they are doing is called masturbating. For example, one young woman I know told me about attending a sleepover where one of the girls was talking about how she masturbated to help her relax. Another young woman said, "Oh, I have to do that all time to go to sleep, but I didn't know that's what it was called."

When a young woman shares with you that she is masturbating, strongly encourage her to seek out community where she can be open about this. She needs to hear that God created a woman's body with a part that gives her pleasure—that it's a gift. She should use that gift in ways that honor God.

Painful Sex

Married women struggle with solutions when sex physically hurts. When that keeps happening, the guy feels like a failure and the woman knows she cannot please him. When a woman doesn't like sex because of the pain, she tenses up beforehand and endures the sex. The pre-sex tension, the painful sex, and the awkward silences after sex start a vicious cycle, and many couples don't know how to stop it. Many avoid intimate conversations about their sexual struggles. When they do talk about the problem, neither is comfortable airing their insecurities. These women feel caught and need someone to talk to about this concern.

When a friend's daughter-in-law was struggling with painful sex, she tried to talk to her mother about the problem. Her mother replied, "Well, your father and I ..." and then went on to talk about their sexual relationship. Bad idea. Being open about sexual intimacy doesn't mean we talk about what we did last night like we're rattling off the events of the day. It's never appropriate to describe your sexual relationship to someone, unless it is a doctor or professional counselor who is trying to help you with a problem. Fortunately, this young woman was able to talk with my friend about the problem, and my friend gently listened and offered to go along to the doctor with her.

My friend did the right thing. If a young woman tells you that she experiences pain when she has sex, encourage her to first see a doctor. The problem may be something physical, such as the presence of the hymen, and a doctor can help. Doctors can be impersonal, blunt, and direct, making them excellent resources when it comes to questions about sex and sexual problems. A good doctor makes the issue about the body and not the person.

Questions about Sexual Terms, Positions, and Related Topics

Despite the seeming openness in our culture when it comes to all things sexual, a surprising number of young women I've met are ignorant of the meaning of certain sexual terms. They often ask me: What is oral sex? What's an orgasm? A clitoris? Why is it sensitive? What does "69" mean? They also have questions about the act itself: Is the girl or the guy supposed to be on top when you have sex? Are other positions normal? Are sex toys wrong?

It's not easy for women to be open with us about such things. It's an honor when they are. Our job is to be prepared for their questions and to have matter-of-fact answers.

Homosexuality

No matter your view on homosexuality or how you interpret Scripture on this matter, you need to know that a percentage of our population is attracted to the same sex. Now more than ever, girls are wondering, *Am I gay?* They think, *I haven't had a boyfriend. I'm twenty-eight. I think about girls sometimes. Am I a lesbian?* A Christian woman who is gay may feel depressed because she's most likely hidden her homosexuality from her parents or others for a long time. She also battles confusion because the church has not helped her walk this road.

As with most sexual issues, homosexuality comes back to identity. *Who am I? Am I loved? Am I enough?* She has a desire to be wanted.[9] Our society says that the more wanted you are, the more valued you are. A young woman struggling with this issue needs to know that the answer to her question "Who am I?" is this: she is beloved by God, a daughter of the King, spiritually formed in Jesus Christ, who is renewing her day by day. You need to tell her this under no uncertain terms. She needs more than just you telling her that she is enough. She needs a community of believers who will help ease the pain of her loneliness so her identity in Christ will be the message she receives.

The Christian community often doesn't know what to do with people who are gay and sends them rejecting messages. If a young woman tells you she is gay—or that she wonders if she is gay—she will be watching to see if you accept or reject her and if you feel awkward around her. If you choose to be gracious, to build a friendship, and to share your life with her, you can help her realize her identity in Christ. Face your fears and sacrifice your agenda of trying to change someone.

Conversations That Restore

I know the idea of having frank conversations about some of these issues may seem daunting, and you may wonder what difference you can make. Let me tell you a story, a confession really, that might help you understand the importance of getting to the place where a young woman is willing to be vulnerable with you.

The sun was just coming up over the Atlantic Ocean when my friend Steph slipped next to me on the bench facing east toward the waves in Ocean City. We were both seventeen years old. "What's going on, Pam? You look pretty bad." I glanced over at the girl who had been my closest friend since grade school and realized she looked just as wiped out as I felt. After searching my feelings so I could put them into words, I started to cry when I spoke.

"I'm done, Steph."

"I think I know what you mean, but what are you done with?"

Like the ocean's waves moments before breaking on the shoreline, the insecurities and loneliness that fed my need for a guy's attention swelled up inside and my heart broke open. "I still feel alone, and I'm tired of pretending that hooking up with a guy for one night or for a week will ease these feelings. Even though we're not technically having sex, being that close to a guy doesn't numb the pain."

"I feel the same way, but how in the world can we ever change? What if we feel alone the rest of our lives?"

As the wind picked up speed off the ocean, blowing my hair across my face, it forced me to smell the mixture of alcohol and smoke. Dark shame, deep guilt, and the sheer feeling of irresponsibility came over me as I confessed, "I need you to see me as the person I want to become. I cannot make this change on my own. I'm a mess and ready to do what I know I'm supposed to do. I just don't feel like I can ever please God. Will you do this with me?"

Steph lowered her head into her hands, took a deep breath, then sat up straight. "I'm so ready, my friend, and I'm with you all the way with this. I'm committed to you. Pam, I want you to hear me. I'm committed to you forever."

Reaching down to pick up our sandals off the boardwalk, we stood up and looked at each other's messy lives and laughed. We put our arms around each other and walked to the car. With our sand-covered feet, empty stomachs, and an Outfield cassette tape playing in the background, we drove west toward home. I knew I'd just experienced my first step toward change, healing maybe. I couldn't put it into words then, but looking back over all these years, what Steph and I did was monumental: we held each other accountable.

Her willingness to go with me, not just in that moment, but also into the next day and the day after that, gave me a safe place to say the truth of who I truly was (sexually broken) and also who I wanted to become. She saw the deepest, darkest, sickest part of me and still loved me. We both knew that following Jesus required us to pursue purity, but we also knew we wanted to follow him out of love—not out of legalism and fear. Steph's ability to love me from her heart propelled me to go higher, further, away from shame to an identity of being renewed by Christ every day.

I'm hoping you will be able to have similar kinds of conversations with the women in your life. Are you willing?

Pay attention for those moments when a young woman is full with questions, confusion, or confession. Those moments are God-given opportunities for you to speak gracious truth from your heart, from a place of love. (For resources and more information about the topics covered in this chapter please refer to my website, www.pamelalau.com.)

Chapter Nine

Building Close Friendships and Working Hard

Listen to your life. See it for the fathomless mystery it is. In
the boredom and pain of it no less than in the excitement
and gladness: touch, taste, smell your way to the holy
and hidden heart of it because in the last analysis all
moments are key moments, and life itself is grace.

Frederick Buechner, *Now and Then*

Friendships and work need our utmost attention in our conversations with the next generation. I would argue that it's in these two places where they experience a lot of private misery.

Whenever I'm talking with young women, they want to know how to have closer relationships and how to have meaningful and balanced work lives. Many say they are unhappy with the quality of their friendships and with the work they are doing. They ask me about my work-ministry history and how it evolved into what I'm doing today. They want something different, but they are unsure about how to get there.

I always begin my conversations about these issues with this question: "How do you want to live?" As we discuss this question, I ask other questions, such as:

- "How would you describe a close friendship?"
- "Do you make time in your schedule to develop closer friendships?"
- "Do you want to work longer hours so that you can pay for the bigger house?"
- "Are you willing to work only from your calling, no matter the cost?"

The answers I hear tell me if they are listening to their lives. Are they making choices that line up with what they say they want in these areas? Or are they saying they want one thing (such as closer friendships) but then making choices (such as working sixty hours a week and communicating with their friends only via social media) that preclude them from experiencing what they want? I've found that if I want to help younger women choose life, I must show them and talk with them about how our choices impact the way we live.

If you've listened to your life and made deliberate choices that line up with what you value and want, then you are positioned to talk about what you have learned and how you have lived your life. Be willing to speak about the strength you've gained from close friendships and the satisfaction you've received through your vocation, whether inside or outside the home.

Developing Close Friendships

When I was twelve years old, I kept a journal with a list of all my closest friends. Beside each name I would draw a portrait of the person and then write words describing what I loved about him or her. As I grew up, my need for friendship didn't change, but I began overfilling my schedule. I wasn't mature enough to ask myself, "How do I want to live?" My life became fragmented, and many of my relationships were superficial. I wasn't listening to my life or trying to find God in everything I did.

Looking back, I can see that while I loved people and knew how to relate to a variety of personalities, I did not make close friendships a priority. Yes, I had many friends, but in my heart I knew something was missing: I lacked deep friendships.

I was in my early twenties when I met a woman who modeled for me what it looks like to make friendship a priority. I witnessed it in LeAnne Lau, my mother-in-law, a woman who was fully alive, fully human, and yet confidently knew her design as a friend to others. The more she nurtured me in the art of real friendship, telling me with her life, *You have a friend in me*, the more I realized I wasn't living the way I wanted to and that I needed to make different choices.

Because a large part of my conversations with young women involves sharing stories from my own life, I often tell them about LeAnne and what I learned from her about what it means to be a friend.

For the first two years of our marriage, Brad and I lived in Colorado near my in-laws. Once or twice a month, we'd drive south on I-25 from Fort Collins for an hour and a half before starting to climb the base of the Rocky Mountains in Evergreen. An hour later, we were breathing beautiful, crisp mountain air where their family home sat on the edge of a cliff overlooking the city. Our weekends spent at Brad's parents' house were filled with games, eating, and just hanging out.

Jerry and LeAnne both taught Bible classes and Sunday school classes with no fewer than one hundred participants. Looking on the outside of their busy lives, many would speculate that their friendships were shallow or that they didn't have time to make relationships a priority. But as a woman who knew the value of friendship, LeAnne didn't let her schedule come before her close friends. I witnessed firsthand how she put first things first in her life every day. She always told me, "Staying close to women is a choice."

Not a weekend passed without several of LeAnne's friends either stopping by or calling on the phone to visit briefly. When I walked into the kitchen while she was on the phone, I often overheard her say, "It's always so good to talk to you. You are [insert encouraging word about that person]. Brad and Pam are here for the weekend, but let's talk again soon." The women in LeAnne's life knew they could depend on her for an encouraging word, a listening ear, or when necessary, a longer conversation.

For LeAnne, prioritizing friendships among her community was the very air she breathed—even when she worked full-time. For eighteen years, my mother-in-law taught communication courses around the country for businesses and government agencies. For twenty years before that, she served as a discussion leader, a teaching leader, and finally an area administrator for Bible Study Fellowship. She was connected to hundreds of women weekly.

She learned early on that without the closeness of women friends, life is lonely, empty, and ultimately self-centered. She did everything to let women know they mattered to her—she wrote cards, made new friends, got involved in her local church, and called her friends on the phone just to check in. Yet in her pursuit of friendship, what made LeAnne stand above the rest in the world of women was that she never felt frazzled. Her love for people did not weary or exhaust her.

As we talked over lunch one afternoon, I asked her about her closest friends. Her eyes sparkled as she described Heidi, Diana, Bev, and Ginger. She listed five more names and then added another three. I knew several of these women and said, "Mom, none of those women are anything like you."

"We have one God in common and he's taught me how to pray for, speak the truth to, and encourage every woman in my life."

Not completely convinced of her approach, I asked her one last question: "How on earth do you find the time for all of these close friendships?"

Placing the white porcelain coffee mug on the table and looking me straight in the eye, she said, "Pam, you and I make choices every day, and prioritizing relationships is a choice to initiate, to be genuinely interested, to be transparent, and to learn to listen."

Her words helped me realize that if I wanted deeper relationships, I had to make space. I decided to back off from a hideously driven life and to slow down. I couldn't have close friendships unless I made time to listen to my friends and be present to them.

My conversations with LeAnne also helped me identify some guiding principles about how to form deeper bonds. These three stand out above the rest:

1. It's not about you. Jesus taught that there's no greater love than to lay down our lives for our friends (John 15:13). When we give up what pleases us to be with a friend or when we set aside time to develop a friendship, we are focused on what we can give to our friend. The invitation to "lay down" our lives for our friends is not a call for us to be people pleasers or to love people more than we love God. When we do these things, our love is self-centered because we are making the relationship all about meeting our own needs. God's path to friendship takes us on a higher road. I understand this when I choose to lay aside my time, my energy, or my to-do list in order to spend time with my friends. However, I find that the more I pray for my friends, the less likely I am to try to fix them or impose on them my own ideas about how they should be living their lives. As I pray for them deeply from my heart, God shows me what they need rather than what I think they want or need.

Recently, my friend Lisa and I couldn't get our schedules to work out so we could get together. This was unusual for us as we try to see each other every day. As my disappointment grew, I started to take the situation personally. I stopped myself as I realized *my* schedule was a problem too. I then prayed for Lisa and was led to drop off flowers on her porch and to wait patiently until we could find another time to connect. When we did finally see each other, Lisa explained the complications on her end. Following God's ways in friendship means praying to find out what our friends need. This turns our selfishness into serving.

2. It's better to outgive. My mother-in-law made the women in her sphere of influence feel like God's most unique creations on their birthdays. She was always sending birthday cards, and each card contained a note written specifically for that friend, based on how LeAnne saw God's design of that one person. LeAnne would list the friend's qualities, noting the impact the person made on her. She would often tell me, "I like to tell the truths that belong to that one person."

Once when talking about a younger colleague, LeAnne said how difficult it was to love her. "Frankly, she's just self-centered. But when I pray for her, I ask God to show me the truth of who she is—what good qualities belong to her. And that's how I encourage her, even though she can be difficult to love." If we're preoccupied with what we receive from a friendship, we are bringing a consumer mind-set into something that money cannot buy. God wants us to give.

3. *If you want deeper friendships, sometimes you have to take the initiative.* I discovered this fourteen years ago when I first moved to the West Coast and met Marcile. We met after she had lost her first husband to a plane crash and married her second husband, Bob. She was sixty-four years old. Marcile had a lot of family members around her, including her eighty-eight-year-old mother, three married children, eight grandchildren, and one great-grandchild. She was the matriarch and didn't indicate she needed any more friends, but we made an instant connection at gatherings, concerts, and celebrations.

I had a deep conviction to meet with Marcile more regularly. It wasn't because she and I had so much in common; our lives didn't reflect each other in any way. But there was something very present about Marcile that I knew God wanted me to witness up close and personal. I had to force myself to ask her to spend time with me at first. But finally I told her I thought she had something to offer me and I wanted to learn from her. We've met on and off for several years.

And I did learn from her. I grew, actually. It wasn't just the Bible studies we did, the books we read, or the prayers we prayed—although Marcile could exegete passages as well as any scholar I've heard. But stepping into her home, just being in her presence, calmed me. It was good for me to set aside my frantic routine of working and driving carpool and to still myself by the window in her room while she sat by me. She was always at peace, and she always wanted to tell me something about her life or herself. I discovered what women so often do in relationships like this one: I sought out the friendship for my sake but kept going for friendship's sake. I met with Marcile because I needed a mentor and ended up becoming her friend. I developed a love for her that runs deep.

When Bob, her husband, died last year, Marcile had to sell their sweet cottage of a home and move into a retirement center. She called me one day and asked if I could come pray with her. As I stood in her doorway, preparing to feel her peaceful presence, I thought about our friendship: It was sweet and endearing. We could be in each other's presence without saying any words. We never ended our time together until we knew the other was encouraged.

Pursuing a friendship with Marcile took courage on my part. I initiated it. If I hadn't, our friendship wouldn't exist. And not only would I have missed out on the privilege of knowing her, but I also would have let pass an opportunity of a lifetime to be a real friend to her. My friendship with Marcile allowed me to pray for more love for her, and God gave me truths that belonged to her—truths about her person that gave so much to me.

Working and Making Money

Along with questions about friendships, young women also ask me about my calling and work life. But what they are all trying to figure out is how their work will support and fit into the lifestyle they desire. Some women want a bigger house in the suburbs while others want little financial pressure so they can travel, serve overseas, or go back to school by living in a smaller home. And if a woman has kids, she may wonder, *Should I cut back on my job or not?*

This was the case for Haley. We began an ongoing conversation about work and making money one evening when a group of friends, including Haley and her husband, were having dinner with Brad and me. We were gathered around a large round table, enjoying light-hearted conversation as we caught up on our families, work projects, and trips. As our food arrived, Haley, who is ten years younger than me, asked, "Pam, how did you decide about making money and working? What informed your decisions?" Haley wanted to talk with a woman who understood the tensions between a woman's working life and her personal life.

One year earlier, Haley and her husband decided they wanted to buy a larger home to accommodate their growing family. His salary was slowly but nicely increasing, which helped support Haley in her artistic pursuits as a freelance photographer. At that time, they could afford their lifestyle and Haley was free to be the primary caretaker of their children. However, they had just found their dream home and were trying to decide what would need to happen for them to be able to afford it. Haley had just realized that she wanted the good life—a life in which she could pursue her passions as a photographer, stay involved with her family, and provide an income to help pay for a bigger home.

This understanding caused her to try to figure out what she could do to make more money. It was forcing her to answer some other critical questions: Do I want to become an employee so that we can live in our dream home? Am I willing to take just any job? How many hours am I willing to work—hours away from my kids? Can I handle the stresses that will come as a result of making this kind of change? If I do get a job, how will it change my calling as a photographer?

Haley wanted to know if my journey had been similar and how I had navigated it.

My single friend Andrea faced a different dilemma: She made plenty of money as a speech therapist but after three years had started to feel miserable and knew she needed to listen to her voice, her vocation, leading her to other work. Before she could just leave a secure job and paycheck, Andrea had to answer some hard questions. On a walk one autumn afternoon, I asked, "What's driving your decision to change jobs?" She answered, "It makes no sense, right? Everyone tells me I have the perfect job. But I'm not happy. I want to live with more free time and not be thinking about my job twenty-four-seven." And then she asked me, "How did you know how to say yes to what you're doing now?" Both Haley and Andrea saw that I was doing work I loved, and they wanted to know how I had accomplished that because they wanted to do something similar.

What Haley and Andrea weren't prepared for me to say was that getting to the point where I could make a living following my passion wasn't as easy as it might look and that I didn't have a formula or specific answers. In the many conversations I had with both of them about this topic, I told them that what I could do was paint them a picture of my working life, my personal life, and the tensions between making money and pursuing my passions. I could tell them about my successes and also my failures—I certainly had made mistakes along the way, including working too little and taking the wrong job before I found my sweet spot, the place where I operate with the most energy. Both had taught me a lot about how I wanted to live.

Talking about vocation and calling in light of all we are discussing in this book is critical: young women are fearful of the future and can feel riddled with comparison of how others are living their lives. If I'm honest, comparing myself with another woman's calling could be the death of me if I'm not listening to the voice of God every single day.

Finding the courage to obey God when it came to my vocation was and is complicated; it's rooted in my sufferings, my friendships, my children, my pleasures, and my talents. Time after time God spoke to the heart of my vocational questions and said, "For by the grace given to me I say to everyone among you not to think of herself more highly than she ought to think, but to think with sober judgment, each according to the measure of faith that God has assigned."[1] There's not much else that causes women more guilt and misery than the comparisons and judgments we make about our or others' working lives. God is so much bigger than the small issues we've made of it all.

So in answer to Haley's and Andrea's questions, I decided to stick to the basics. I told them a few of the lessons I'd learned in my working life to give them a picture of what I had done that had allowed me to get to this point. I share a few of them here so that you can do something similar in your own conversations with the young women in your life.

The Value of Getting a Varied Experience

In high school and college, I took any job I could get to help pay for gas and also to help pay for my college tuition. Working in various positions, especially with the public, gave me diverse experiences and helped me clarify what I wanted to do for work as an adult.

One day in May of 1990, my dad drove down to Lynchburg, Virginia, to help me pack up my college dorm room before driving me back home to New Jersey. Dad valued hard work and didn't waste any time in finding out when I was going to get a job. I was thinking if I had a job by the end of the summer, I was doing pretty well. I was also pondering my applications for grad school when my dad asked me, "What are your plans to work?" I had just been offered an interview for a full-time job as the local advertising manager at a Gannett newspaper in Cherry Hill, New Jersey. I knew it was an awesome opportunity to get experience, but I was torn because I also wanted to pursue other jobs or a graduate degree. What my dad understood then that I did not was that getting experience and working hard mattered more than getting the perfect job.

My dad made it clear that I needed to make money and pay my own way now that I had finished college. I wanted to go to grad school, but didn't have the money to pay for it. So the next morning, I was able to arrange an interview, which led to a job offer for a position with a salary, full benefits, gas money, and a chance for promotion.

Because I took this job, I learned the value of earning my own money and I learned how to work hard. The month after I took the job, a fellow employee became very sick and had to leave his job in national sales. My boss offered me the job as the national advertising manager, which quickly increased my pay and my responsibilities. The job felt too big for me, but after weeks and months of long hours, stressful decisions, and learning new concepts, I began to realize that I was doing my best. And that felt good.

On top of that, I loved my job as national advertising manager. I met people from all over the East Coast, and it provided me with professional experience that would be recognized in the workplace. Having that job gave me a sense of autonomy and the satisfaction of supporting myself. Being able to pay my bills and have money to do what I wanted gave me a sense of great accomplishment and worth as a worker. These were God's gifts to me in that season because exactly one year later, my decision to get married took me in a different direction.

When the women in my workplace heard I was getting married and leaving my position, they promptly told me I was making a big mistake after all I had invested in my job. My career, they insisted, was more important than a relationship with a man. This caused me some angst, and I told a few women from my church about it. They responded, "But doesn't it feel good to not worry about working so hard anymore?" Both responses were offensive to me. I was tempted to stop sharing with the Christian women in my life and to stop listening to the women at my work. I knew that I didn't want to put my work above everything else in my life. That was not how I wanted to live. But I also loved working and couldn't imagine my life without it.

The Value of Doing Our Best

When Brad and I decided to attend graduate school in Colorado, I left my job in New Jersey, only to land in a city where professionals were waiting tables for a living. I had to force myself to apply for jobs at a temp agency. I wouldn't have minded, but I had just left a great job and felt this was taking a step back. My first temp job was to sit at a front desk and answer the phone for a company that manufactured plastic parts. Every morning the boss showed me the flow chart of the organization, pointing with his large, fat finger at the bottom, where my name was. I lasted about two weeks. My second temp job for the local electric company wasn't much better. I sat in a cubicle and took pictures of residents' monthly electric bills and filed them. I did this for eight hours a day.

One day the general manager came to my cubicle and said, "Pam, I hear you want to write. How would you like to go out on assignment and write for our magazine? We will pay you hourly above and beyond your current job." I learned a valuable lesson about making money and working: taking the temp jobs, doing work that didn't fit with my passions, working wholeheartedly in a job when the boss asked me to do menial tasks like getting ice every morning for his Diet Coke were stepping-stones that gave me varied experiences and taught me to do my best, no matter the job. Even when I was writing articles on the rising costs of electricity, a topic I didn't care about, I gained satisfaction from learning something new and doing my best.

The Value of a Meaningful Life

A few years later, I earned my graduate degree and accepted a full-time position as an English professor. After I had our third child, I had to decide whether to continue working, as the cost of full-time child care would significantly diminish my ability to add to the bottom line of our family income. Although my husband was a terrific and involved father, his career made it impossible for him to share in the child care. Again I had to ask myself, "How do I want to live?" I answered that question by deciding that the financial bottom line wasn't as important as the little people who were being added to our family. I wanted to revolve my life around people differently; I was becoming more interested in a meaningful life, not money. I had to ask myself if I was willing to hire a nanny or find full-time child care. Could I handle the constant pressures of work and small children? What were the consequences of stepping out of my career this soon?

I decided, with Brad's support, to leave my profession because I could not care for three babies and pay attention to my work at my fullest capacity. I tried it for a while, and all I could produce everywhere I went was frantic and anxious work. So I made a decision based on how I wanted to live and then made adjustments. Easy enough, right?

Wrong.

Living by Your Values Brings Challenges

The adjustments were painful. We sold our home in the suburbs and rented a shoe-box-sized townhouse near the college where Brad worked. It was an abrupt downsizing. On top of that, my decision to stop earning money felt like a choice to stop pursuing my vocation and to downsize our lifestyle. Even with good intentions of investing my time more in relationships, I had a hard time structuring my life without a "job."

A year or so later we bought another home by cashing out my 401(k). As our family grew, so did our expenses and my desire to work again. What I wasn't prepared for was how my capacity for making money had shifted. My lifestyle of having three small children and a husband with a high-profile job required everything of me. I was not capable of taking on full-time work, so I took a job that offered me quarter-time work and was eventually able to increase my hours to half-time, helping us reach our financial needs from month to month. For a few months, everything fell into place and it felt good to be in a better state financially. But I was starting to feel miserable. I was in my midthirties and no longer wanted to work just in order to pay the bills. That wasn't enough for me anymore; I knew God was leading me through my dissatisfaction. But where was he leading me?

One thing became clear: I could not compare my working life with the working lives of other women. I waited for God to show me his divine plan for me. In that waiting time, I learned that every choice I made had consequences. But I wasn't left on my own in making those choices if I was willing to listen and wait.

Once again I was faced with the question of how I wanted to live. Did I want to work to pay for our vacations and visits to our families? To have my girls attend private school? How important was making money to me? Or did I want a job that gave me the flexibility to work differently? I started to ask if I could work for myself. Did I have the discipline?

Over time I discovered my calling by noticing that people kept coming to me with the same questions and problems and by realizing that I had a burning desire to show them how God had helped me with those same questions. I saw many spiritual needs but couldn't meet them unless I made some changes. This insight led me to make significant life choices about my vocation so I could have a job that was more in line with my calling. But honoring my true self while living within the confines of our financial reality was not easy.

When that first month came around and there wasn't enough money to cover the school tuition, we transferred two of our girls to another school. They missed their friends, teachers, and the smaller school so much that they became unhappy. I knew I had to stick with my decision, so I worked even harder to earn money doing what I loved so I could help my girls go back to their school. Within five months, I had not quite enough work to be able to send them back, but the financial aid office at the school helped make up the difference. Staying true to my calling was never so hard as it was those few months, because the people I loved the most were sacrificing for my choices. But I learned how to let others step into my calling with me, sacrificing any notion that I was doing this on my own. And as things came back together, I felt more settled knowing I was living how God wanted too.

Share Your Own Stories

I struggled with writing this chapter because there's no nice way to tie this all together and wrap it up beautifully. There are no cut-and-dried answers for us to give to the women behind us—but we do have our experiences.

After twenty-five years of working different jobs, I had the skills and the reputation to work on my own as a writer and speaker. What many younger women don't have is the perspective of how much time and experience it takes before you are ready and able to make a decision like that.

If you're honest about your own history, you may find you can identify with my story. Your perspective on friendships and work and what you've learned are stories younger women need to hear, even if you are still trying to figure things out yourself.

Perhaps you are working on building friendships. Ask yourself what happened in your life that made you aware of your desire for real friends. And if you have years of history with friends, ask yourself, What has made those friendships tick? What makes a good friend? Or maybe you've stopped making friendships a priority and you need to ask yourself why. Did you experience disappointment too many times? Do you believe women are just too difficult to love?

Ask yourself, How has God led in my decision to work or not to work for money? Have I accumulated more debt than I can pay off in a few months? Are profits or people more important to me? How do I know? Have I taken my calling seriously enough to move toward fulfilling it? If not, why?

Our goal is to encourage young women to take a step back and ask, What kind of life do I want to have and what kind of life does God want me to have? It's important we know how we ourselves would answer those questions as we talk about our varied friendship and work experiences. And remember, in preparing how you would answer younger women, you are becoming a safe haven on relevant issues about which the church has remained relatively silent.

Chapter Ten

Loving Well So Others Can Truly Live

The first thing to prosper should be inside of me.

TobyMac, "Lose My Soul"

The year our daughters were eight, six, and five, they found a box of kittens at our neighbor's moving sale. The sign on the box read "Free." They brought the kittens home, and our garage was transformed into a kitten paradise. The girls spent every waking moment caring for and playing with the cats. I explained that we couldn't keep them, and when the kittens were old enough, we took them to the humane society. Actually, I had to pay the humane society to take the kittens. About a week later, we discovered the kittens at our local pet store. Annalise, then six years old, instantly found her kitten, Sally, and for an hour played with her furry friend. As I was loading the girls back into our van, I suddenly heard a shrill scream, "I want my cat!"

Lying prostrate on the sidewalk, cars whizzing past, Annalise continued to scream, "I want my cat!" She was stiff; I couldn't peel her off the sidewalk.

My cell phone rang; it was Brad asking me why I was late. In exasperation I relayed the scene and heard the heart of a father, "Buy her cat back." I was silent. He said it again, "Her heart belongs to that cat. Buy her back the cat." I placed the phone on Annalise's ear, and Brad repeated to her what he told me. She picked herself up and I hung my head as I walked back into the pet store and wrote the check for the kitten I had just a week earlier paid the humane society to take! (Disclaimer: you could see this as a weak moment for my husband, but for the sake of the story, let's focus on his heart!)

Days later I heard our youngest daughter say to her sister, "You know what, Annalise? I like the heart better than the head. Remember when you wanted Sally back and Mom said, 'No, Annalise, it makes no sense to buy your cat back,' but then Dad heard you crying and he said, 'Pam, her heart belongs to that cat.' See, I like the heart better than the head." My daughters had discovered one of the most important truths: love lies at the center of their father's character.

A Call to Love the Next Generation

I see women just like you and me who want the same confidence in knowing our heavenly Father's love. Like Paul's call to the Philippians in his second chapter, this book is my call for women to open wide their hearts so God's love can pour through to the next generation of women. *The Message*'s rendering of verses 1–4 mirrors the passion of my heart:

> If you've gotten anything at all out of following Christ, if his love has made any difference in your life, if being in a community of the Spirit means anything to you, if you have a heart, if you *care*— then do me a favor: Agree with each other, love each other, be deep-spirited friends. Don't push your way to the front; don't sweet-talk your way to the top. Put yourself aside, and help others get ahead. Don't be obsessed with getting your own advantage. Forget yourselves long enough to lend a helping hand.

That's a powerful call, and one we can answer only when we make a radical decision never to compromise the qualities of God's love for our own agendas or comforts.

What holds us back from living out the love of God? Life gets long. Our relationships and our circumstances can leave us cynical, unbelieving, and tired. After years of investing in relationships, we may be left in the muck and mire of disappointment, no longer confident in God's love. The enthusiasm we once felt in our faith has led to disillusionment or apathy.

But when we give ourselves totally to God, it keeps us alive in our faith.[1] It convinces us that God's love is more powerful than what the world offers. I believe the more you and I know for ourselves God's loyal love in the depths of ourselves, the more able we will be to model and teach it to others.

God's Unfailing Love

According to the Old Testament, the word that describes the center of God's character is *hesed*. In Exodus 34:6–7, God gave a confessional to Moses: "The LORD, the LORD, a God merciful and gracious, slow to anger, and abounding in steadfast love and faithfulness, keeping steadfast love for thousands, forgiving iniquity and transgression and sin" (ESV).[2]

Hesed refers to God's multifaceted, extravagant, unfailing love. It's a best love usually reserved for close friends and family members, but the act of hesed can be shown in any relationship. Hesed is a love that comes from someone who is superior and stronger and with feelings beyond loyalty. R. C. Sproul Jr. said the best translation of hesed love would be "loyal love."[3] God loves his people genuinely, immovably, and loyally. With hesed love, both love and loyalty are intertwined. God cannot be loyal without love. In other words, God will never stop being *for* his people.

My girls understood this about their father's love, and I pray they will live it out for others. But what restored Annalise's spirit that day she was lying prostrate on the pavement were her father's words, "Buy her cat back." As we give ourselves totally to God, immersed in his promises to us, we won't just teach and model God's love to the younger women; we, as my husband did to our daughters, will become God's living and loving word to this next generation.

Let me share with you some things I've learned about loving with hesed love—about being merciful and kind, slow to anger, abounding in steadfast love, and committed to the next generation for the long haul.

Merciful and Kind

I remember the evening we had company for dinner and my two-year-old daughter, Gabrielle, wanted a snack. Rather than ask me for one, she dragged the stool to the pantry, stood on top of it, pointed, and screamed. Everyone laughed. But I knew deep down something wasn't right.

Gabrielle was small and blonde, anxiety ridden, and the youngest of three girls born close together. People explained away her speech difficulties by saying, "Everyone else talks for her; that's why you can't understand her."

I could understand Gabrielle. As long as I stayed close to her, what she wanted became known to me. Sorrowing for her to be understood, I answered for her, raced to her side, and tried to protect her from the pain of other kids turning away when they couldn't understand her. I wanted to be her relief.

After twelve months on our own without progress, I called the local school for help. Mercy walked through our front door. When Barbara, a highly intuitive and talented speech therapist, worked with Gabrielle, she also worked with me. Her mercy and kindness changed our lives.

Four times a week, Barbara gave me specific skills to support Gabrielle. She had to learn to pronounce her *d*'s, *t*'s, *s*'s, and *b*'s at the beginnings and ends of words. Once Gabrielle could sit still long enough for me to whisper a word in her ear, she could repeat it properly and her spirit came to life. After she learned several consonants clearly, they started to run together and she could speak sentences like running water.

It was not possible for Gabrielle to have language without someone teaching her with a merciful and kind spirit; she was dependent on such kindness. Barbara modeled for me how mercy and kindness act: they stoop down to a person's level. Barbara's actions remind me of the way David described what God did for him: "You give me your shield of victory; you stoop down to make me great" (2 Sam. 22:36).[4] Barbara taught me that if my attempts to help Gabrielle lacked mercy, lacked kindness, she would never learn. Did my face reflect mercy? Were my eyes filled with kindness?

As I held my daughter close, we spent hours face-to-face, cheek-to-cheek, my mouth to her ear, while we sounded accurate tones for *a*, *b*, *d*, *t*, *st*, and *p*. Back and forth, back and forth…. This was my sacrifice: I used my body language to show my daughter that I didn't feel stressed or burdened or rushed. I slowed my speech so as not to rush while I was in her presence. Barbara modeled for me how to do this. She didn't hold back her knowledge, her resources, or her skills—mercy sees the person's need and draws close with a best love, a genuine love, a humble love. Isn't that what safe havens are for?

Barbara's influence in my life changed the way I showed love to my daughters—and to all younger women in my path. When a student, Megan, offered to help me with computer problems after one of my lectures, I invited her back to my office. While she worked on my computer, I was chatting away about my latest project when she stopped and said, "Pam, I have no idea what you mean when you talk about Scripture. I want to know God and everything, but you lost me."

I looked at this precious young woman as my heart filled with love for her, and I started over. I stooped down in my heart. "Tell me, Megan, what part doesn't make sense to you?" With mercy and kindness, I looked into my young friend's face and talked about Scripture with one thought at a time. To this day, Megan and I share a loving relationship because she knows my love for her meets her exactly where she is. That's hesed love.

Slow to Anger

I'm deeply thankful that God describes his love as slow to anger as opposed to saying he has no anger. Passionate Christ-following women can have so much zeal that we can come across as angry and frustrated. A wise person once told me I wasn't angry, I just knew when something wasn't right.

In my desires to love the women closest to me with a hesed love, I look to Jesus and am deeply moved by how Scripture describes him. When the rich young ruler knelt before Jesus and begged to know what he had to do to inherit eternal life, Jesus engaged in a theological conversation with him. Mark wrote that before Jesus corrected the young ruler's problem of relying on his possessions, "Jesus looked at him and *loved him*" (Mark 10:21).

Jesus spoke lovingly to the man's heart. Because Jesus didn't express frustration and because he loved the young man before he answered him, the man laid bare the true state of his heart. Jesus never compromised his heavenly Father's love. Similarly, when I love as God loves, the Holy Spirit fills me with loving responses, even in situations when my anger flares up. It's not always easy for me to show mercy and kindness; it's an area in which I plead with God for help. The times I've grown the most are when I've been angry with someone and the Holy Spirit has filled me, equipping me to love that person and respond with kindness.

Even when we disagree with someone, it's possible to model and teach, without constant frustration, what God's love is like—slow to anger, forgiving, accepting. This may sound spineless to some. But when we refuse to cooperate with our impatience and pride, we show others how we care about them, which will result in them being encouraged that God is active in their lives and helping them get ahead.

A few years ago, I was teaching a student who needed professional help for her special needs beyond what a private school could offer. When several conversations with her young mom proved useless, I turned to my administrators for help. For several weeks, they tried to help the mom see how serious her daughter's needs were, to no avail. Word got back to me that this mom was gossiping about me and blaming me for the disruption in her daughter's education. I was furious.

I organized a meeting with the administrators, the mom, a few colleagues, and myself for the following week. Preparing for this meeting, I made careful notes of the events and how I would confront the mom, when suddenly the Holy Spirit spoke to my heart, saying, "Pam, you are to remain silent until I tell you to speak." That made me mad too! But the following morning in the meeting, I was silent as I listened to the discussion. About fifteen minutes in, one of the administrators asked another teacher a question about the student. After the teacher answered, the mom sat up straight and said, "Why haven't you ever told me this before?" The room fell silent, and the mom turned to me and said, "Pam, you were trying to tell me this but I refused to listen." Eventually, the student was transferred to another school and given the help she needed. The mom found me later and said she was surprised that I hadn't come against her in anger, especially in the meeting. I was tempted to rehash how much time, energy, and conversations were wasted while her daughter learned nothing for two months. But God's love slowed me down. I placed my hand on her arm and said, "I'm thankful your daughter is in a much better place. How is she feeling about the changes?" And with that, the mom filled me in on all the details, emphasizing how much her daughter was learning with the right help.

I learned a lesson from this about the role of frustration in my life: it can give me clues to help solve a problem, but it should never be in charge of the solution. Slowing down our anger is always the right thing to do. What good would I have accomplished if I held on to it? Love, especially God's love, doesn't push itself to the top. When I didn't compromise by trying to get my own way, God's love did the impossible.

Are you slow to anger? If you're a mom of young children, you may be feeling frustrated with me for even suggesting it's possible! I know how that feels. When we radically decide to love others well, we will not be perfect. It's all preparation for what's coming next in our lives. We will have flashes of anger and frustration. And when we do, we can own them and ask for forgiveness. I think I've asked my own daughters to forgive me ten thousand times. The more we experience and know that *God is for us*, that his loyal love is for his people, the greater our chances are of becoming his slow-to-anger love for those closest to us.

Steadfast

The meaning of God's steadfast love came home to me when I met Dorothy. Standing five foot three inches tall with short brown hair and piercing blue eyes, Dorothy at first comes across as mild mannered and quiet. In reality she is direct and razor-sharp intentional about her words. We met at the weekend retreat in Bellingham, Washington, where I was speaking. The director of women's ministries introduced her to me as "an intercessor." Dorothy modeled a constant, consistent, loyal love for the women at the conference, and she offered that same steadfastness to me—a stranger, really—by writing me cards, asking me what my requests were, and praying in a room by herself while I was speaking.

Several days after the conference, I contacted Dorothy to thank her, and she asked how she could continue to pray for me. That was more than five years ago, and she has remained true to me in an unlikely partnership for life and ministry. Once a week we connect by phone and pray for the week, my schedule, any upcoming events, my family, and protection in our work. This may seem simple, but Dorothy's consistency and insistence that we do this regularly has grounded me in an appreciation for commitment. In between our weekly connections, she sends me texts, asking specifically about a few items from my list. Because her motives are to see God's work in my life and in the world, she is a steadfast safe haven for me.

I'm not the only one to whom Dorothy demonstrates this kind of steadfast love. Several other women in her life benefit from her gifts of prayer, kind notes, thoughtful acts of service, and friendship too. Her presence has been a deep source of encouragement as it reflects the reality of God in my life. What I mean is that since we are both committed to Christ and his Word, our commitment to each other has a greater meaning, a larger purpose; it's not just for ourselves.

I'm convinced that I might have missed many promises of God without our consistent prayer time. Even more important, Dorothy's modeling of steadfast love has taught me how to do the same with a few younger women in my life. The world's systems make it easy to concede to being unfaithful in relationships, to be halfhearted in commitment. I strongly encourage you to go against the tide and be steadfast in your love for other women.

Committed for the Long Haul

In the fall of 2010, I found myself in a dark and sad time, unable to deeply feel the love of God in my life. Through unusual circumstances, my family and I had left a supportive community where we had been highly involved for seven years. Landing in a new one was hard, but we did. Feeling disconnected, I asked God to show me more of himself in this new group of people. I even had several friends constantly checking in with me, but I struggled with feeling loved and could not erase the emptiness from all we had lost. Yet as the following story shows, God demonstrated his commitment to me and to another woman.

I was in a meeting when I heard the following announcement: "Please pray for Sarah and Ben as their mom didn't show up yesterday to pick them up from school." As the next several days unfolded, the story grew in complication.

Tonya was a single mom who had her own business. She was a biologist who traveled around the country training other biologists. Her husband had been arrested on criminal charges and imprisoned, and he had left behind mounds of debt for Tonya to pay off on her own.

On a September afternoon, while Sarah and Ben were waiting after school for their mom, Tonya apparently had a stroke at home.

A friend found her hours later after being contacted by the school to come pick up the children.

"She is in a coma," I heard at the next meeting. "Let's do whatever we can for this woman; she is new to our community."

I sensed God leading me, and a day later I stood in Tonya's hospital room.

Lying on the hospital bed, Tonya had tubes, wires, a catheter, a lung machine, and a heart monitor attached to her. She had a nine-inch scar from one ear to the back of her shaven head, where the doctors had done surgery in order to stop the bleeding in her brain. Cheryl, her sister, told me how she and Tonya were raised in an upper-middle-class family in Washington. Their father was a successful engineer, and Tonya was a strong student who graduated from college with honors. Cheryl said, "Things got really bad these past few years, and Tonya didn't let anyone but us know how serious the problems really were—with her marriage, their finances, and her children. On the phone, Tonya would often tell me, 'I just can't let anyone know what's really going on.'"

A few days later, while Tonya was still in a coma, some friends and I traveled into Portland to visit her. I called Cheryl to let her know we were coming.

"Pam, you're not going to believe this, but for the first time since the stroke, she is awake!"

We rode the elevator to the third floor and entered the hospital room. The air was putrid, but the sight trumped the nauseating smell: Tonya's eyes were open. Immediately, I slid to her side and held her hand. "Tonya, you don't know me, but I teach at Sarah's school. Your daughter and son are going to be fine. But we are here to tell you that God loves you so much. He is crazy for you to know that his love for you is so powerful. We drove over an hour to tell you this today." The surge of love flowing through me to this woman was undeniably divine and of a power outside my own.

"Tonya, can we pray for you?" asked my friend.

Tonya squeezed my hand. Still dizzy over the fact that this woman was awake, we asked God for Tonya's healing; we prayed for her body, her brain, and her lungs. I stepped aside for a moment to look out the window as I was just so overcome by God's fierce love for this woman whom none of us knew.

"Tonya," asked my friend, "would you like to accept Jesus Christ into your heart so you can spend eternity with him in heaven?"

I stepped back to the side of the bed as Tonya grabbed my hands and lifted them both straight up in the air. We had just witnessed heaven intersecting with earth in a cold, sterile, smelly hospital room. The joy was palpable.

Outside the room, Cheryl asked if Tonya was up and walking around with all that noise. She confided to us later that she didn't know where she stood with her faith, but she knew something happened that day in her sister's hospital room.

A week later, Tonya passed away. The only people present at her funeral were immediate family members and a few friends. Cheryl stood in front of the small group and talked about her sister's life. She ended with the question that was on everyone's mind: "With all of the technology that kept Tonya's physical body alive when her major organs started shutting down, where was the machine to carry her deepest burdens?" I answered quietly to myself, "Jesus. He became what she needed in those last hours. He was committed to her to the very end, keeping her eternally safe."

Tonya's story stays with me. It lives with me. I was only in her world for less than a few weeks, but in that short time I realized that God did not allow this precious woman, a leader in her field, a loving mother, an outwardly together and intelligent creation of God, to take her last breath without knowing how fiercely he loved her. And then I realized that God had used Tonya's life to show me how much he cared about me too.

During the time I was involved with Tonya's situation, the women in my life kept telling me, "Pam, let me know what I can do for you or for her." God cared about Tonya, and at the same time he cared about me. With only my empty heart as a carrier to reach out to Tonya, God filled me with divine love for a woman no one knew was in such trouble, and he touched her soul. My friends did what women do best in times of crisis—they came alongside me, prayed for me, prayed for Tonya, and made food for her children and her brother. Whether or not it was sensible, showing Tonya how much God cared about her while she was dying renewed my heart because I became "absolutely convinced that nothing—nothing living or dead, angelic or demonic, today or tomorrow, high or low, thinkable or unthinkable—absolutely *nothing* can get between us and God's love because of the way that Jesus our Master has embraced us" (Rom. 8:38–39 MSG).

Give Yourself Totally to God

I believe in what God's love does and what God's love says. As you give yourself totally to God in dealing with your suffering and cry out for him to search you, he will reveal what's in your heart. As you offer the power of healing comfort with the comfort you have received, he will sing over you. As you stand at a crossroads with someone in dire need, God will spark your heart as you act with understanding. When you know him as full Forgiver, it cleans your heart, positioning you to help someone else to know redemption too. As you offer someone shelter by relating to her with compassion, you are showing the world you have a heart that cares, that you are a deep-spirited friend, and that you can love another person well so she can live.

Today the church talks about the love of God as something we must show to the world. The pendulum in Christian culture has swung once again to the side of knowing God's love as opposed to knowing his Word. Our calling is to reflect the reality of hesed love. Loyal love stays true to the Word of God and to the people of God. What the world and women are longing for is hesed, a love that is as binding as family—something that equals commitment. Our loyalty and our love are toward what we believe and to those with whom we believe.

Love restores. Love repairs. Love supports. Love encourages. Hebrews 3:13 reminds us to "encourage one another daily." That call is still for you and me today. Love lies at the center of God's character, and every time we answer the call to love women well, we become safe havens for them—this is what comforts them, encourages them; this is what makes us happy and sets our hearts free. What are we waiting for?

Keeping Your Heart Clean

I learned early on that I had to provide space for myself to keep my heart clean. It may sound strange, but seeing forgiveness as a choice has shaped who I am today. I've learned to allow some time, maybe once a week or a handful of times a month, to have down days or down hours to be by myself for the purpose of being with God, for the purpose of practicing forgiveness and cleaning my heart from bitterness, anger, or self-pity.

To keep your heart clean, schedule a day or half day in a quiet place so that you can be still. Stillness is not loneliness, isolation, or cloistering yourself away and avoiding relationships and community. Stillness is being alone in God's presence and listening to God in silence. Once you are quiet, here are some spiritual movements you can try for your heart:

Read and reflect on Isaiah 30:15, a passage often used for quiet days: "In repentance and rest is your salvation, in quietness and trust is your strength." You may find you resist being still without something to occupy your mind. Ask yourself why you are resisting the gracious presence of God. Sometimes I realize I avoid being still because I reason to myself that I can just handle my heart issues by myself. Or I admit I just don't have the time. I've learned it's a necessity for me to be still to know forgiveness and to grow spiritually.

Silence helps us cease from striving. When my girls were young and still took naps, I used that time to write my first book, *Soul Strength*. For some women that would not seem like a ceasing from striving, but for me it was the best form of silence I could take during those months. I shut off my phones, invited the Holy Spirit to guide me, and wrote what I was learning from Scripture. A woman who needs to keep her hands busy to remain silent might choose to cook in her kitchen or organize her files or tinker with her technology. The purpose is to let your mind relax without needing to speak aloud. Do whatever it takes to quiet your mind. For me, building with words all by myself is my best form of silence, and it allows me to quickly hear what my heart has to say. How long you are silent is entirely up to you.

Thanksgiving is inviting. If the purpose of having quiet is to invite God into a time when we want to forgive and be forgiven, then how we talk to God matters. If you invited a friend to your house, you would welcome her in, make her feel at home, thank her for coming, and be kind. I often say to God, "Thank you. Thank you for the breath in my lungs and this new day. Thank you for being a God who hears and who knows the number of hairs on my head." Making a mental list of gifts from God in your life and in the world saturates your heart with an attitude of reverence. God is the source of all life, and since you are preparing your heart to forgive or be forgiven, reminding yourself that all good things come from him will help you remember that he will give you a heart of forgiveness too.

Self-examination is the hard part. Ask the Holy Spirit to search you and know you as you linger in his presence. Keep in mind that nothing is hidden from God. He longs for you to bring your grievances to the surface. Start confessing from your heart. Express all of your feelings, knowing the purpose of this is to clean your heart. Ask him to expose any anger or bitterness you may feel for sins done to you. Truth brought to light brings healing. Confession is good for the soul. By doing this, you are showing a dependence on Jesus as Healer, because through the Holy Spirit, any grievances will be exposed.

Receiving forgiveness starts with repenting for your sins. Tell God about the people involved and the situation. Write or pray how this situation made you feel and how it demands or demanded too much from you. Pray for God to forgive you and for his help to forgive those who have hurt you. Can you forgive yourself for separating yourself from God's love or from another person's love?

Request what you need from God. Pray from your knees and see yourself as a daughter asking her father for a favor. Kneeling shows reverence and deference. Asking dissolves self-reliance. What are you asking God for? Do you need him to fill you with his love for people? Do you need love for a person who offended you? Do you need to forgive yourself? One of the gifts we quickly get from quiet days is seeing how God fulfills our requests. Because the person you must forgive failed to meet a need you had, it's important that you ask God to meet that need. It forces you to name the need.

Write it out. We can live with pockets of guilt and shame for weeks, years, and decades. If you must, write a letter to someone asking for his or her forgiveness or extending forgiveness. I will often write the letter first to read what I need to say and then meet with the person face-to-face.

Note: for more resources like this, please go to www.pamelalau.com.

Acknowledgments

I could not have written *A Friend in Me* without the help of numerous friends, family members, and colleagues, including Heidi Mitchell, my agent, who believed in this project from our first interactions even more than I did. Our countless discussions, emails, and questions over the past two years caused me to see her as a partner in this message—she believed in it that much. If it were not for Marty Raz being at the right place at the right time, I never would have met any of the wonderful people at DCJA, including Don Jacobson and Blair Jacobson.

It has been a privilege to work with Ingrid Beck and the team at David C Cook: Tim Close, Darren Terpstra, Karla Colonnieves, and Jack Campbell. They invested their talented resources in a message others wanted to take on but were afraid of the risks. Thank you for championing this book. Liz Heaney has to be the most talented and dedicated editor in the industry. She wasted no time in finding my faulty reasoning and underdeveloped points while at the same time believing that I had something powerful to say. Liz's insights are what make this book clear. My heartfelt thanks to you, Liz. This book wouldn't be complete without your hard work.

Thanks to Katelyn Beaty and Kate Shellnutt at *Christianity Today*'s Her.meneutics for posting the first two blogs about this issue and to Pam Jacobs at Barna Group for pulling up questions and data on churchgoing women.

A handful of dedicated people read the entire manuscript, offered detailed suggestions, and spent hours talking through specific concepts. These include: Meredith Dougherty, Adrienne Ochs, and Donna Buhrow (Donna helped me understand the theology behind John's gospel and Psalm 119). Another group, with the help of David Sanford, read through early versions of chapters and offered insights. They are: Lisa McMinn, Catherine Johnson, Olivia Pothoff (who also composed the beautiful music for "Hold Me Close"), Melanie Mock, Judie Buddenbaum, Colleen Sump, Susan Hubbard, Stephanie Nelson, Shari Scales, Sheri Philips, Sonja Yoder, MaryKate Morse, Melanie Dobson, Kelly Bard, Barb Baylis, Valerie Sjodin, Lee Ann Zanon, Jenna Brown, and Jen McCourt.

I'm grateful to Elisa Fryling Stanford for her skilled guidance and to Laura Barker for her encouragement.

A special group of women prayed tirelessly for me in the early years of this book, encouraging me to write in the light what I heard in the dark. My heart will forever be grateful for Melissa Chimento, Heidi Farner, Kelley Kanyer, Laurie Rauch, Karen Reinhardt, Lecia Retter, Toni Williams, Kathy Kambic, Michelle Bervik, and Stephanie Hendricks. Angela Bayford prayed words of life about this book, helping me see the next step. Lisa Church, Jillian Willis, Susan

Ninteman, Tiffany Raugust, and Dayna Lemke prayed and showed love when I didn't even know how to ask, and Laurie Sheffield talked for hours with me about chapter 6. And when we weren't finished talking, she would call me from her car and then text with me late into the night.

I relied on the participation and encouragement I received from the women who participated in my interviews and attended our Shaping Her Faith conversation. Cindy Streimer opened her home, and I'm so thankful for the women who came: Janette Stoltzfus, Denise Pia, Vida Ice, Sarah Baldwin, Kayin Griffith (who was an integral part of forming chapter 8), Amy Widmer, Shannon Weiss, Terra Mattson, Toni Day, Rachel Hoffman, Jamie Sharp, Dee Ann Hutchins, Katie Yates, Carolyn Hulbert, Brianne Emel, Kaitlin Thomas, Marta Sears, Kathie Nelson, Beth Clark, Marcile Crandall, Laurie Charbonneau, Brianne Hansen, Lanae Phelps, Karin Engleman, Jennifer Garrick, Amy Karjala, Heidi Oliver, Chelsea Moore, Caitlin Davis, Sarah Hoffman, and Julia Terman.

I owe a great deal to Chelsea Smith, who worked hard in helping me with videos, taping, and assisting in various ways to help get this message formed. She started out as a student and has become my friend. And to Rob Westervelt, who graciously answered my questions even after long conversations. Kevin Dougherty found the exact statistics I was looking for on a day no one could help me. Rick Muthiah responded quickly in an emergency and rescued me from computer craziness. Shannon White and Zeeyad Farrouge creatively produced the videos for each chapter.

Writers need places, and the George Fox University library was the perfect place for me to write—thanks to Jane Scott for always going the second mile. Richard Silver and Marlee Zakrevsky at print services showed patience time after time.

I am deeply thankful for LaNeal Miller who stood by me when I needed support and gave me space when I needed to write: she consistently offered me the highest form of friendship—my life is richer because of her.

I owe a great debt to Dorothy Borneman for faithfully praying for me and for this book for more years than she bargained for. She modeled God's steadfast love from miles away. Her ministry humbles me.

Most of all I thank my family: Tom Havey and LeAnne Lau both spent extensive time in our home during the writing of this book and never once made me feel guilty for hiding away. LeAnne's influence in my adult years went above and beyond the role of a mother-in-law. Rebecca MacDowell opened her heart and her life. And to Sandra Goldstein, my mom: I'm so thankful that God is the Restorer of our relationship.

And to my beloved husband, Brad, and our three daughters, Michaela, Annalise, and Gabrielle, who are the most patient and kind people on earth. My girls told me at least once a week, "Mom, I believe in you." Brad cheered me on, read chapters of my book, wouldn't let me even think of quitting when things got hard, and showed me constant support until the last hour. Your love is endless and I will never get over how crazy in love I am with you. May each of you know you always have *a friend in me*.

For my heavenly Father, the Lord Jesus, and the precious Holy Spirit, thank you for loving me. May all glory and splendor and honor be yours alone.

Notes

Chapter 1: A Young Woman's Longings

1. Christian Smith et al., *Lost in Transition: The Dark Side of Emerging Adulthood* (New York: Oxford University Press, 2011).

Chapter 2: Safe Havens

1. David Kinnaman, *You Lost Me: Why Young Christians Are Leaving Church ... and Rethinking Faith* (Grand Rapids, MI: Baker Books, 2011), 118.

2. This is a paraphrase of Jung's "All haste is of the devil." See Aniela Jaffé, *From the Life and Work of C. G. Jung* (Am Klosterplatz, Einsiedeln, Switzerland: Daimon Verlag, 1989), 132.

3. Annie Dillard, *The Writing Life* (New York: HarperCollins, 1989), 25.

4. Donald S. Whitney, *Spiritual Disciplines for the Christian Life*, rev. ed. (Colorado Springs: NavPress, 2014), 15.

5. Tim Herrera, "The More You Use Facebook, the Less Happy You'll Be: Study," *Newsday*, August 15, 2013, www.newsday.com/news/new-york/the-more-you-use-facebook-the-less-happy-you-ll-be-study-1.5899902.

6. This quote is from the 1984 edition of the New International Version of the Holy Bible.

Chapter 3: The Other Side of Pain and Suffering

1. "Jesus answered: 'Watch out that no one deceives you'" (Matt. 24:4).

2. "My goal is that they may be encouraged in heart and united in love, so that they may have the full riches of complete understanding, in order that they may know the mystery of God, namely, Christ, in whom are hidden all the treasures of wisdom and knowledge" (Col. 2:2–3).

3. The book of Deuteronomy.

4. See Job 5:18; Psalm 103:10–14; Proverbs 3:12; Isaiah 48:10; Lamentations 3:33; Hebrews 12:5–6; and 1 Peter 5:6.

5. C. S. Lewis, *The Problem of Pain* (New York: Macmillan, 1962), 81.

6. "Remove the dross from the silver, and a silversmith can produce a vessel" (Prov. 25:4).

7. "God has said, 'Never will I leave you; never will I forsake you'" (Heb. 13:5).

8. See 1 Chronicles 29:11–12; Psalm 97:1–6; Habakkuk 3:19; Romans 9:21; and Ephesians 1:11–12.

9. "My goal is that they may be encouraged in heart and united in love, so that they may have the full riches of complete understanding, in order that they may know the mystery of God, namely, Christ, in whom are hidden all the treasures of wisdom and knowledge" (Col. 2:2–3).

10. Nicholas D. Kristof and Sheryl WuDunn, *Half the Sky: Turning Oppression into Opportunity for Women Worldwide* (New York: Alfred A. Knopf, 2009).

11. Kenda Creasy Dean, *Almost Christian: What the Faith of Our Teenagers Is Telling the American Church* (New York: Oxford University Press, 2010), 139.

12. Philip Yancey, *Prayer: Does It Make Any Difference?* (Grand Rapids, MI: Zondervan, 2006), 221.

Chapter 4: The Power of Comfort

1. Dan Kimball, *They Like Jesus but Not the Church: Insights from Emerging Generations* (Grand Rapids, MI: Zondervan, 2007).

2. David Kinnaman, *You Lost Me: Why Young Christians Are Leaving Church … and Rethinking Faith* (Grand Rapids, MI: Baker Books, 2011), 21.

3. Christian Smith et al., *Lost in Transition: The Dark Side of Emerging Adulthood* (New York: Oxford University Press, 2011), 151.

4. Catherine Marshall, *The Helper* (Waco, TX: Chosen Books, 1978), 136.

5. Kenda Creasy Dean, *Almost Christian: What the Faith of Our Teenagers Is Telling the American Church* (New York: Oxford University Press, 2010), 3.

6. Pam Lau, "To Christian Women under 40: We're Sorry," Her.meneutics, August 2013, www.christianitytoday.com/women/2013/august/to -christian-women-under-40-were-sorry.html.

7. Barna Group found that two-thirds of evangelical women over forty describe themselves as deeply spiritual, compared to about half of those under forty. Although 47 percent of young women do not see themselves as deeply spiritual, they still consider themselves leaders. They are more likely than us, their mothers and their grandmothers, to take on these leadership roles. This study was conducted by Barna Group in April 2010 and included telephone interviews with 603 women who described themselves as Christian and had attended a Christian church service at least once in the past six months. Data analyst Pam Jacobs provided this information for me.

Chapter 5: Acting with Understanding

1. Gary Cross, "Jaded Children, Callow Adults: What We Lose When We Expand Adolescence," *Chronicle of Higher Education*, March 10, 2014, http://chronicle.com/article/Jaded-Children-Callow-Adults/145117.

2. Joan D. Hedrick, *Harriet Beecher Stowe: A Life* (New York: Oxford University Press, 1998).

3. Eugene H. Peterson, *Leap over a Wall: Earthy Spirituality for Everyday Christians* (San Francisco: HarperSanFrancisco, 1997), 82.

4. Erwin Raphael McManus, *Chasing Daylight: Seize the Power of Every Moment* (Nashville: Thomas Nelson, 2002), 10–11.

Chapter 7: Relating with Compassion

1. Through Joseph, the Lord brought seventy individuals into the land of Egypt (Exod. 1:1–6). The people became numerous (v. 7) in the midst of suffering (vv. 8–12) and were led out of Egypt as a large multitude of about two million people (12:37–38).

2. Henri J. M. Nouwen, Donald P. McNeill, and Douglas A. Morrison, *Compassion: A Reflection on the Christian Life* (New York: Doubleday, 1983), 4.

Chapter 8: Conversations about Sex

1. "What I'm really trying to say is I want the deepest, darkest, sickest parts of you that you are afraid to share with anyone because I love you that much." On the November 2, 2009, episode of *It's On with Alexa Chung*, Lady Gaga said this concerning the lyric "I want your psycho, your vertigo shtick/Want you in my rear window, baby you're sick" in her song "Bad Romance" (*The Fame Monster* © 2009 Interscope Records).

2. See Proverbs 5:19; Song of Songs 5:10–16; and 1 Corinthians 6:17; 7:3–5.

3. Timothy Keller and Kathy Keller, *The Meaning of Marriage: Facing the Complexities of Commitment with the Wisdom of God* (New York: Dutton,

2011). See chapter 8, "Sex and Marriage," for an excellent discussion of this topic.

4. See Genesis 2:24; Psalm 63; 1 Corinthians 6:17–20; and Ephesians 5:31.

5. In Galatians 2:20, Paul said he had been crucified with Christ. It didn't mean he had no personality, personal goals, or interests. What trumped all those was "Christ who lives in me" (ESV), leading and directing him moment by moment. Living in Christ is our most powerful identity.

6. First John 3:1, 3, and 6 don't teach sinless perfection, but they do indicate that a child of God will stop sinning habitually to please God. It's our job to keep reminding the young women of their position in Christ. Once they truly know Christ, they will want to live pure lives.

7. See Deuteronomy 33:12; Song of Songs 2:16; Ephesians 1:3–6; and 1 Peter 2:9.

8. I talked extensively with Kayin Griffith, formerly the assistant director of spiritual life, inclusion, and student leadership in the spiritual life department at George Fox University for seven years. She and her colleagues interacted with students regularly about this issue.

9. I spoke in depth with Kayin Griffith about this issue as well. See previous endnote.

Chapter 9: Building Close Friendships and Working Hard

1. This is a paraphrase of Romans 12:3 (ESV).

Chapter 10: Loving Well So Others Can Truly Live

1. Caleb was who he was at the end of life because he gave himself totally to God (Josh. 14:6–12).

2. See also Nehemiah 9:17, 31; Psalms 86:15; 103:8; Joel 2:13; and Jonah 4:2.

3. R. C. Sproul Jr., "What Is Hesed?," Ligonier Ministries, May 4, 2013, www.ligonier.org/blog/what-hesed/.

4. This quote is from the 1984 edition of the New International Version of the Holy Bible.